A study of the hymnic and liturgical material in the New Testament which describes Christ's nature and person. Professor Sanders analyzes the hymns in detail and finds in them a common mythological pattern. He traces its origin to a particular and unorthodox branch of Judaism which is itself a branch of the 'wisdom' tradition where the thanksgiving hymn had its home. His conclusions therefore have considerable importance and implications for questions about the origins of Gnosticism and its influence on Christianity.

This is the first full-scale historical religious study of the New Testament Christological hymns, and English readers will find particularly useful Professor Sanders' critical survey of recent continental scholarship on this and related subjects.

SOCIETY FOR NEW TESTAMENT STUDIES
MONOGRAPH SERIES

GENERAL EDITOR
MATTHEW BLACK, D.D., F.B.A.

15

THE NEW TESTAMENT
CHRISTOLOGICAL HYMNS

THE NEW TESTAMENT CHRISTOLOGICAL HYMNS

THEIR HISTORICAL RELIGIOUS BACKGROUND

BY

JACK T. SANDERS

Associate Professor of Religious Studies
at the University of Oregon

CAMBRIDGE

AT THE UNIVERSITY PRESS

1971

Published by the Syndics of the Cambridge University Press
Bentley House, 200 Euston Road, London N.W.1
American Branch: 32 East 57th Street, New York, N.Y.10022

Library of Congress Catalogue Card Number: 70-123670

ISBN: 0 521 07932 2

Printed in Great Britain
at the University Printing House, Cambridge
(Brooke Crutchley, University Printer)

TO MY MOTHER
AND
IN MEMORY OF MY FATHER

CONTENTS

CONTENTS

PREFACE

The problem of the origin of Gnosticism is a knotty one. The History of Religions School, including the New Testament scholar Rudolf Bultmann and his pupils, sees Gnosticism as a religious movement coming into and influencing Christianity. Others point out that such a supposition is built from texts which are no earlier than the second century A.D. The History of Religions School replies that since there are gnostic concepts in early Christianity, including the New Testament, these concepts must have come into Christianity from somewhere, i.e. from Gnosticism. Opponents of this view reply that there are no pre-Christian texts supporting such a view. It is to one aspect of this problem that this study seeks to address itself.

A basic premise of this inquiry should be expressed here at the outset. It is simply this, that the concepts found in the New Testament material that will be discussed here were not created *de novo* by the Christian community. Heinrich Schlier made this point most succinctly in 1930 regarding the term 'new man' in Eph. ii. 15.[1] The fact that the author employs this term without any explanation renders it improbable that it 'sprang from his fantasy'. Nor can the term be explained as an interpretation of Pauline statements like those in Rom. v. 12 ff. and I Cor. xv, since it would still have to be explained how the Pauline 'second man' could become the 'new man' of Eph. ii. 15, a term which seems to involve rather a different set of concepts. The point is that this, and the other mythical concepts that will concern us here, in all probability had their origin in pre-Christian religious circles. To define these circles as accurately as possible is the purpose of this work.

I wish to express my most sincere appreciation to my former *Doktor-Vater*, Professor James M. Robinson, who provided invaluable advice and criticism of this work in its several stages prior to submission as a Ph.D. dissertation at Claremont in 1963, and who also read and commented upon the revised manuscript prior to publication. My thanks go also to Professors

---

[1] Heinrich Schlier, *Christus und die Kirche im Epheserbrief* (Beiträge zur historischen Theologie, 6) (Tübingen, 1930), p. 27.

PREFACE

Ernest C. Colwell and Eric L. Titus, who also advised me
during the preparation of the dissertation. Grateful thanks are
further due to Professor Matthew Black and the Syndics of
Cambridge University Press for accepting the work for publication in this series, as well as Professor W. D. Davies and
Dr R. McL. Wilson of the editorial board of the series, who
read the manuscript and called to my attention several important writings I had otherwise overlooked. Needless to say,
responsibility for any errors or mistakes of judgment will have
to rest with me alone.

The original writing of the dissertation was made possible by
a National Defense Education Act Fellowship, and the revision
by an Emory Summer Research Award; I am deeply indebted
to the Department of Health, Education, and Welfare of the
United States Government and to Emory University for these
grants. Special thanks go to Mrs Pauline E. Pullen of Atlanta,
Georgia, who turned some almost impossible copy into a
beautiful typescript.

J. T. S.

Eugene, Oregon
October 1969

ABBREVIATIONS

BZNW	Beihefte zur *Zeitschrift für die Neutestamentliche Wissenschaft*
CBQ	*Catholic Biblical Quarterly*
EvTh	*Evangelische Theologie*
FRLANT	Forschungen zur Religion und Literatur des Alten und Neuen Testaments
HNT	Handbuch zum Neuen Testament
ICC	International Critical Commentary
JAC	*Jahrbuch für Antike und Christentum*
JBL	*Journal of Biblical Literature*
JBR	*Journal of Bible and Religion*
JerT	Jerusalem Targum
JTS	*Journal of Theological Studies*
NTD	Das Neue Testament deutsch
NTS	*New Testament Studies*
PRE	*Realencyclopädie für protestantische Theologie und Kirche*
RB	*Revue Biblique*
RGG	*Die Religion in Geschichte und Gegenwart*
RHPR	*Revue de l'histoire et de la philosophie religieuses*
RNT	Regensburger Neues Testament
SBT	Studies in Biblical Theology
TDNT	*Theological Dictionary of the New Testament*
ThLZ	*Theologische Literaturzeitung*
ThR	*Theologische Rundschau*
TWNT	*Theologisches Wörterbuch zum Neuen Testament*
VChr	*Vigiliae Christianae*
ZNW	*Zeitschrift für die Neutestamentliche Wissenschaft*
ZThK	*Zeitschrift für Theologie und Kirche*

EDITORIAL NOTE

Except as noted, all English quotations of the Old Testament and of the Apocrypha are from the Revised Standard Version of the Bible and of the Apocrypha respectively, copyright 1952 and 1957 by the Division of Christian Education of the National Council of the Churches of Christ in the United States of America, and are used by permission. Quotations of the New Testament in English are those of the author, except those noted RSV, which are from the Revised Standard Version of the Bible, copyright 1946, and also used by permission. Grateful acknowledgment is also made to Walter de Gruyter & Co., Berlin, for permission to print the table on pp. 84–5, and to Professor Helmer Ringgren, Uppsala, for permission to use the transliterations and translations of Ras Shamra texts on pp. 51 f.; further, to Rascher Verlag, Zurich, for permission to quote from the English translation of the Gospel of Truth, and to the John Rylands Library, Manchester, for permission to quote from the English translation of the Odes of Solomon (see footnote 3 on p. 44).

HYMNS IN THE NEW TESTAMENT

When one thinks of hymns in the New Testament, one thinks first perhaps of those that have been traditionally used by the church. Thus the *Magnificat* (Luke i. 46 ff.), the *Benedictus* (Luke i. 68 ff.), the *Gloria* (Luke ii. 14), and the *Nunc dimittis* (Luke ii. 29 ff.) come to mind. There is also some express hymn singing in Revelation.[1]

For some time, however, there has been an awareness in some circles that the New Testament contained other hymnic materials. Joseph Kroll, in 1921, began working in the direction of a study of New Testament hymnody by analyzing and characterizing other early Christian hymns.[2] Building on the earlier philological work of Eduard Norden,[3] Kroll pointed out the festive, emotional, and dramatic character of Christian hymnody.[4] More important, he attempted to distinguish hymns from prayers and confessions. Thus, although both hymns and prayers may be characterized by thanksgiving and petition,[5]

---

[1] Cf. for example Rev. iv. 8–11; vii. 10–12.

[2] Joseph Kroll, *Die christliche Hymnodik bis zu Klemens von Alexandreia. Verzeichnis der Vorlesungen an der Akademie zu Braunsberg im Sommer 1921* (Königsberg, 1921; reprinted Darmstadt, 1968).

The subject matter of this introduction, and of ch. 1, has now been treated extensively and admirably by Reinhard Deichgräber, *Gotteshymnus und Christushymnus in der frühen Christenheit. Untersuchungen zu Form, Sprache und Stil der frühchristlichen Hymnen* (Studien zur Umwelt des Neuen Testaments, 5) (Göttingen, 1967). As this work only became available to me in the final stage of preparation of the MS of the present work, it was impossible to deal with Deichgräber's evidence and conclusions in the thoroughgoing manner that would seem to be indicated. The more important aspects of his work, however, especially agreements and disagreements, are taken account of in the footnotes, with his reasons. At this point, particular note should be made of the thorough treatment of the history of the formal study of early Christian hymnic materials given by Deichgräber, pp. 11–21.

[3] Eduard Norden, *Agnostos Theos* (Stuttgart, 1956[4]; originally written 1912). Norden had pointed out, in particular, the use of *relative clauses* and *participial predications* in liturgical texts. Cf. particularly *ibid*. pp. 168, 221 f. He distinguished between oriental predications (including those translated into Greek), which have substantive participles, and truly Hellenic predications, which have predicative or attributive participles (*ibid*. pp. 202 f.).

[4] Kroll, pp. 11, 78.   [5] *Ibid*. p. 10.

Kroll saw hymns as displaying more 'ardor of enthusiasm' than prayers, and as being more formally constructed.[1] If this is a rather generalizing distinction, and one feels that one still could not always distinguish between a hymn and a prayer, this feeling is intensified somewhat by Kroll's distinction between confessions and hymns. 'A confession-like formula', he suggests, 'can very easily have its place in a hymn...Thus a hymn can receive an expressly doctrinal character.'[2] Nevertheless, Kroll saw confessions as distinct from hymns in that a confession is regularly characterized by an 'enumeration of the data of salvation'.

This general usage of the word 'hymn' to indicate a religious song, which usage is carried over into the more recent discussions of liturgical materials in the New Testament, is not thoroughly considered;[3] yet it is possible that the use of the term 'hymn', comparable to the precise form-critical usage of the term in Old Testament research to designate one *Gattung* of psalm, may ultimately be applicable here in equally as precise a way. Hermann Gunkel designated one of the four major *Gattungen* of psalm the 'hymn', calling it also a 'song of praise'.[4] A hymn normally began, as he saw it, with the plural imperative 'praise', 'sing', or 'thank', and the body of the hymn recounted the deeds or gave the attributes of God. Claus Westermann, who has directed some criticism at Gunkel's position,[5] prefers the term 'psalm of praise' to 'hymn',[6] and distinguishes between 'descriptive praise' and 'narrative praise', referring the former term to most of the passages Gunkel had designated 'hymns' and the latter term to those passages placed by Gunkel in the category of 'thanksgiving song'.[7] Westermann devotes particular attention not only to the 'thanksgiving' category of psalm, but to the concept, to the phenomenon of thanking as well,[8] finally finding in the phenomenon of thanking an understanding of existence in which man

---

[1] *Ibid.* p. 11.   [2] *Ibid.* p. 16 n. 2.

[3] It was so for the New Testament period also, of course; cf. Eph. v. 19: 'speaking to one another in psalms and hymns and spiritual songs, singing and psalming in your heart to the Lord, giving thanks always...'; cf. also Col. iii. 16. On the varied use of the term 'hymn', cf. Deichgräber, p. 21 n. 3.

[4] Hermann Gunkel, 'Psalmen', *RGG*, edd. Gunkel and Leopold Tzscharnack, vol. IV (1930[2]), cols 1612–14.

[5] Claus Westermann, *Das Loben Gottes in den Psalmen* (Göttingen, 1961[2]).

[6] *Ibid.* pp. 17 ff.   [7] *Ibid.* p. 23.   [8] *Ibid.* pp. 17–21.

knows himself to be in need of God.[1] This interest in the thanksgiving psalm and its relation to the hymn proper is maintained by Georg Fohrer in his Old Testament introduction.[2] Fohrer follows Westermann in separating the thanksgiving from the hymn, but notes that 'hymnic motifs are frequently employed in the explanation [of the thanksgiving]'.[3] Fohrer keeps the terms 'hymn' and 'song of thanks'. Following the opening call to thanksgiving, according to Fohrer, the body of the song of thanks recounts a previous situation of need, and how God saved from that need. The conclusion of the thanksgiving psalm, as is the case with the hymn, then repeats in some way the praise given at the beginning.[4]

It seems likely that this *Gattung* of thanksgiving psalm (or 'narrative praise'), so closely related to the *Gattung* 'hymn' (or 'descriptive praise') as to be at times almost indistinguishable, is the *Gattung* to which most of the New Testament passages to be discussed here belong. In this regard,[5] James M. Robinson seems to have shown fairly clearly the existence in early Christianity of the liturgical formula, 'I thank thee, Lord, for...', followed by two lines giving the cause for thanksgiving. The prayer of thanksgiving itself then followed these two lines, and this prayer could become more or less hymnic, so that Robinson can refer to 'hymnic prayers of thanksgiving'.[6] Some of the 'prayers' following the characteristic introductory thanksgiving formula are so obviously poetry or liturgical songs, however, that Robinson refers to them as 'hymns'.[7] The two examples of this phenomenon are Rev. xi. 17 f. and Matt. xi. 25–7 = Luke x. 21 f. Of these passages, Robinson says, 'Where it is simply a matter of inspired singing, precisely here the *hodayoth* formula turns up intact'.[8] He also takes

[1] *Ibid.* p. 53.

[2] Georg Fohrer, *Einleitung in das Alte Testament*, begründet von Ernst Sellin (Heidelberg, 1965[10]).   [3] *Ibid.* p. 290.

[4] Regarding the relation between thanksgiving and hymn, cf. further Deichgräber, pp. 21–3, who agrees in general with Westermann.

[5] James M. Robinson, 'Die Hodajot-Formel in Gebet und Hymnus des Frühchristentums', *Apophoreta, Festschrift für Ernst Haenchen*, edd. W. Eltester and F. H. Kettler (BZNW, 30) (Berlin, 1964), pp. 194–235.

[6] *Ibid.* pp. 213–21.   [7] *Ibid.* pp. 226–35.

[8] *Ibid.* p. 226. His reference to 'inspired singing' of course recalls the festive, emotional, and dramatic character of Christian hymnody to which Kroll called attention, and the 'ardor of enthusiasm' present in hymns.

Col. i. 12 ff. to be an early Christian hymn on the same pattern,[1] seeing in the words, 'giving thanks to the father', in *v.* 12 an allusion to the characteristic *hodayoth* formula, and in *v.* 13 the characteristic two-line designation of the cause for thanksgiving:

Who has delivered us from the power of darkness
and transferred us to the kingdom of the son of his love.

Following this mention of the son come the words, 'In whom we have redemption, the forgiveness of sins' (*v.* 14), which 'completes the transition to Christ';[2] and then follows the Christ 'hymn' of *vv.* 15–20. One will note the rather close formal similarity between Col. i. 12–20, as Robinson explained the formal structure of the passage, and the description of the 'song of thanks'—one *Gattung* of psalm—given by Fohrer. At the beginning is a call to thanksgiving, and this is followed by a recounting of a situation of need and how God saved from that need (by means of the cosmic drama described in *vv.* 15–20).

Thus it seems that the designation of at least this passage as 'hymn' in Gunkel's usage, as 'narrative praise' in Westermann's terminology, or as 'song of thanks' in the description given by Fohrer would be justified. As the *Gattung* represents, for the Old Testament at least, one type of psalm, the designation 'thanksgiving psalm' would also be appropriate. Since the New Testament writers (Col. iii. 16; Eph. v. 19) apparently made no distinction among 'psalm', 'hymn', and 'thanksgiving', the term 'hymn', which is the word normally used today for religious songs, seems to be appropriate as a general designation for referring to all such passages.[3] The formal relation of the other passages to be discussed here to Col. i. 12–20 and to the *Gattung* 'hymn' (or 'thanksgiving psalm') will be indicated in the analysis following.

One element of early Christian hymnody to which Kroll called attention was the dramatic character and the 'ardor of

---

[1] *Ibid.* pp. 231 f.   [2] *Ibid.* p. 233.
[3] Thus Deichgräber, who basically distinguishes between 'hymn' and 'prayer' (prayers of petition and of thanksgiving), recognizes the rather indefinite line between hymn and thanksgiving and does not at all mind using the designation 'hymnic' in the broader sense in which 'hymn' is used here; cf. *ibid.* pp. 22 f., 47.

enthusiasm' common to hymns.[1] It may be noted here, however, that this is not merely a stylistic or formal observation, but refers as well to the *content* of the hymns, since early Christian hymnody tends to deal with a divine *drama*, a cosmic redemption, thus with an 'exalted' subject.

[1] See above, pp. 1 f.

PART 1

FORMAL ANALYSIS OF
THE HYMNS

CHAPTER I

THE NEW TESTAMENT CHRISTOLOGICAL HYMNS

PHILIPPIANS ii. 6–11

6 Who, Being in the form of God,
　　　Did not think it robbery to be equal with God,
7　　But emptied himself,
　　　Taking the form of a slave.

　　　Becoming in the likeness of men
　　　And being found in fashion like a man
8　　He humbled himself,
　　　Becoming obedient unto death
　　　　　　[the death of the cross].

9　　Wherefore God highly exalted him
　　　And bestowed upon him the name above every name,
10　　That in the name of Jesus every knee may bow
　　　in the heavens and on earth and beneath the earth,
11　　And every tongue confess,
　　　'Jesus Christ is Lord!'
　　　　　　to the glory of God the father.

The arrangement given here is essentially that of Joachim Jeremias.[1] Ernst Lohmeyer had earlier arranged the passage strophically into two stanzas of three strophes each, each strophe containing three lines having three stresses each.[2] Since this arrangement involved placing only one finite verb in each stanza, and since the analysis took account of the numerous participles and emphasized the consciously structured character

---

[1] Joachim Jeremias, 'Zur Gedankenführung in den paulinischen Briefen', *Studia Paulina in honorem Johannis de Zwann*, edd. J. N. Sevenster and W. C. van Unnik (Haarlem, 1953), pp. 146–54. Cf. the earlier designation of the form of the hymn as *zweigliedrig* by Rudolf Bultmann, 'Bekenntnis- und Liedfragmente im ersten Petrusbrief', *Coniectanea Neotestamentica*, vol. XI (1947), p. 6 n. 10. Cf. further Deichgräber, pp. 118–33.

[2] Ernst Lohmeyer, *Kyrios Jesus. Eine Untersuchung zu Phil. 2, 5–11. Sitzungsberichte der Heidelberger Akademie der Wissenschaften*, Phil.-hist. Kl. (Jahrgang 1927/8, 4. Abhandlung; reprinted Darmstadt, 1961).

of the passage, Lohmeyer's arrangement remains widely
accepted.[1] The insistence of Jeremias, however, that the passage
is structured along lines of Semitic *parallelismus membrorum* seems
more adequately to explain the structure of the passage, at least
for *vv.* 6–8. Jeremias pointed out that the two lines of *v.* 6 should
be seen as parallel, as well as the two lines of *v.* 7*a*, *v.* 7*b*, and
v. 8. By omitting the words 'in the heavens and on earth and
beneath the earth' in *v.* 10 and 'to the glory of God the father'
in *v.* 11, Jeremias gained two more pairs of lines exhibiting
parallelismus membrorum. He then claimed that the three stanzas
thus produced presented respectively the pre-(earthly) existence, the earthly existence, and the post-(earthly) existence of
the redeemer.[2]

That this division of the passage into three stanzas, giving
three stages in the existence of the redeemer, is the correct
division can hardly be doubted, Lohmeyer and the verse
enumerations notwithstanding. Not only can *vv.* 6–8 be seen to
contain four pairs of parallel lines, but the two stanzas are in
fact built on the same pattern. The first line of each stanza
begins with and ends with a participle, and gives the state or
'place' of the redeemer in either case. The second line in either
case then explicates what was said in the first line; this is done
synonymously in the second stanza ('likeness' = 'fashion', 'of
men' = 'like a man') and complementarily in the first stanza.
'Humbled himself' is the equivalent in the second stanza to
'emptied himself' in the first;[3] and the fourth line of each

---

[1] Cf. Ernst Käsemann ('Kritische Analyse von Phil. 2, 5–11', *Exegetische Versuche und Besinnungen, Gesammelte Aufsätze*, vol. I (Göttingen, 1960), p. 52), Günther Bornkamm ('Zum Verständnis des Christus-Hymnus Phil. 2, 6–11', *Studien zu Antike und Urchristentum, Gesammelte Aufsätze*, vol. II (Beiträge zur Evangelischen Theologie, 28) (Munich, 1959), p. 178). That *vv.* 6–11 are quoted by Paul at this point seems adequately to have been demonstrated by Lohmeyer, pp. 4 f., who called attention to the 'strongly unified and... carefully formed' aspect of the passage, as well as to the way in which it follows abruptly on *v.* 5, and who pointed to the wealth of participial predications; and by David M. Stanley ('The Theme of the Servant of Yahweh in Primitive Christian Soteriology and its Transposition by St Paul', *CBQ*, vol. XVI (1954), p. 421 n. 97), who lists the *hapax legomena*.

[2] Jeremias, 'Zur Gedankenführung in den paulinischen Briefen', pp. 150–4.

[3] Lohmeyer, incidentally, in his commentary (*Die Briefe an die Philipper, an die Kolosser und an Philemon* (Kritisch-exegetischer Kommentar über das

stanza, like the second line, explains the preceding line by giving the new state of the redeemer. Even those two designations (the fourth line of either stanza) are comparable: 'slave', 'obedient'.[1]

A passage exhibiting such a structure of lines and stanzas might be called simply a poem and not a hymn; but to these observations regarding structure one may add observations of a liturgical nature. Thus one may note that the presence of an abundance of participles and the general absence of the article throughout most of the passage point to a liturgical setting for the poem,[2] as does the likely allusion to a doxology at the end of the passage.[3] If one would normally refer to a liturgical poem as a hymn in a general sense, the opening relative (ὅς) and the closing doxological allusion probably indicate a more precise setting for the hymn, i.e. as a hymnic expansion of a thanksgiving[4] and thus probably justify the designation of this passage as a 'hymn' in a precise sense.[5]

If Jeremias' analysis of the strophic arrangement of *vv.* 6–8 seems to be correct, Lohmeyer's arrangement of *vv.* 9–11 will

NT) (Göttingen, 1964 (= 1930)), pp. 94 f.), saw that lines one and three of what is Jeremias' second stanza were analogous to lines one and three of what is Jeremias' first stanza; but his own strophic arrangement, of course, prevented his drawing the correct implications from these observations. This evidence is overlooked by Deichgräber, p. 124, who, by relating ἐκένωσεν (against Jeremias) to the incarnation, opts for a twofold division.

[1] Jeremias followed Lohmeyer in omitting the words 'the death of the cross' as being a Pauline addition to the quoted material. Lohmeyer, *Kyrios Jesus*, p. 44, had argued that the qualifying involved in the phrase 'unto death' of the absolute subjection and humiliation as the lowest stage of existence brings, by emphasizing the *type* of death, a discordant note to the theme of the passage. This view is widely accepted and is certainly correct.

[2] Cf. the information given by Norden, above, p. 1 n. 3.

[3] Cf. Phil. i. 11 and my earlier discussion of this phenomenon in 'The Transition from Opening Epistolary Thanksgiving to Body in the Letters of the Pauline Corpus', *JBL*, vol. LXXXI (1962), p. 357.

[4] Or of a blessing, which is an alternate form to the thanksgiving, and was finally entirely replaced by the thanksgiving in Christianity. Cf. Robinson, p. 204; further, A. D. Nock, 'Hellenistic Mysteries and Christian Sacraments', in *Early Gentile Christianity and its Hellenistic Background* (New York, 1964; originally published 1952), p. 134. Deichgräber, however (pp. 124 f.), though recognizing the possibility of such a setting, pronounces a '*non liquet*' over 'the question regarding the original wording of the beginning', and conjectures Ἰησοῦς, Χριστός, κύριος, or even αὐτός as the original for which ὅς now stands. [5] So also Deichgräber, p. 118 n. 4.

hardly be the original one. But Jeremias' arrangement of these verses also leaves something to be desired. Not only is there a change of subject at *v.* 9, but the two elements that so strongly characterized *vv.* 6–8 as hymnic, absence of the article and wealth of participles, are precisely missing in these last verses, with the exception of the acclamation and doxological ascription of praise at the end; but the doxological final line was omitted by Jeremias.[1] There is the further problem that *vv.* 9–11 rely heavily on an Old Testament passage, Isa. xlv. 23 f., something which is not the case for the first two stanzas. Thus, if the original formal structure of *vv.* 6–8 seems accurately to have been reconstructed, this is not quite the case for *vv.* 9–11; and perhaps the original has been enough changed in these verses, by Paul or by the congregation from which he learned the hymn, to prevent a thoroughly accurate reconstruction of the original.[2]

COLOSSIANS i. 15–20

15 Who is the image of the invisible God, first-born of all creation,

18*b* Who is the beginning, the first-born of the dead, [that he himself might be pre-eminent in everything]

16 For in him was created everything in the heavens and on earth, [the visible and the invisible, whether thrones or lordships, whether rulers or authorities] Everything was created through him and unto him.

19 For in him all the fulness was pleased to dwell,

20 And through him to reconcile everything unto himself.

[1] Georg Strecker ('Redaktion und Tradition im Christushymnus Phil 2, 6–11', *ZNW*, vol. LV (1964), p. 70) has argued for a division into two stanzas, dividing between *vv.* 8 and 9. Although this solution is in some respects tempting, it fails to make adequate use of the now obvious formal structure of *vv.* 6–8.

[2] On the possibility of pre-Pauline additions in *vv.* 9–11, cf. also Deichgräber, p. 126.

17 And he is before everything,
   And everything is united in him,
18 And he is the head of the body [the church].

The arrangement given for this passage—except for the bracketed material, which he omitted—is that of Eduard Schweizer.[1] This arrangement has the advantage of making the greatest possible capital out of what had already been emphasized by James M. Robinson in his earlier study of the formal structure of the passage[2]—that is, that there are elements in either of what appear to be two stanzas here that have analogies in the other stanza. Schweizer has merely placed these analogous portions of the passage side by side, has omitted all material not having an analogy in the other stanza, and has attributed *vv.* 17 and 18*a* to a middle stanza which falls out of the pattern of analogous construction. He has followed Robinson in omitting the final words of *v.* 20, 'making peace through the blood of his cross, through himself, whether things upon the earth or things in the heavens', as being those of a redactor. If Phil. ii. 6–8, with its analogous construction of two stanzas, may be taken as a clue, then Schweizer's reconstruction of the original hymn here is perhaps proceeding in the proper direction. Others are certain to stumble, however, over the volume of the omissions; thus, Robinson's reconstruction of the original, which does not omit quite as much material as Schweizer's, would still seem to be worth considering. Robinson suggests only two stanzas (thus avoiding Schweizer's awkward middle stanza); and, by the transposition of certain lines, on the basis of a comparison of the passage with Col. ii. 9 f., he was able to maintain the analogous structure of the two stanzas throughout.

Although the original formal structure of this passage may never be fully explained,[3] enough is evident to allow the modern

[1] Eduard Schweizer, 'Die Kirche als Leib Christi in den paulinischen Antilegomena', *ThLZ*, vol. LXXXVI (1961), col. 241.

[2] Robinson, 'A Formal Analysis of Colossians 1: 15–20', *JBL*, vol. LXXVI (1957), pp. 270–87. Norden, pp. 251 f., had already pointed to the corresponding elements.

[3] This is about the opinion of Deichgräber, p. 150. Deichgräber proposes as possible an original structure that proceeds directly through from *v.* 15 to *v.* 20, in content very similar to the reconstruction of Robinson. Also in agreement with Robinson, Deichgräber (p. 151) conjectures only two

reader to see at least in general what that structure was. When one then notes—in addition to the hymnic aspects in the introduction[1]—the presence of predicative relative clauses and of the ὅς, comparable to that in Phil. ii. 6, opening each stanza, then one may recognize the validity of the statement of Ernst Käsemann that 'the hymnic character of Col. i. 15–20 is long since recognized and generally accepted'.[2]

EPHESIANS ii. 14–16

[For] he is our peace,

Who has made both one
And has broken down the dividing wall of the fence [the enmity],

In order to make the two into one new man in him [making peace],
And to reconcile both in one body to God [through the cross].

This reconstruction of the original strophic arrangement of Eph. ii. 14–16 attempts to be minimal rather than definitive.[3] Gottfried Schille first recognized the hymnic character of the passage,[4] but he wished to include in the hymn the quotation of Isa. lvii. 19 in *v.* 17. It seems unlikely, however, that anything after *v.* 16 belongs to the quoted hymn; and the references to 'the enmity' (*vv.* 14 and 16) are so closely related to the theme of this section of Ephesians that it seems probable that they are interpretive additions by the author. *V.* 15*a*, 'having abolished in his flesh the law of commandments in ordinances', included by Schille and placed in parallel position to 'who has made both one and has broken down the dividing wall of the fence' creates the difficulty that the latter clause seems rather to be *two* lines which themselves exhibit *parallelismus membrorum*, as indicated

original stanzas, beginning at *v.* 15 and *v.* 18*b*. In view of the repeated ὅς ἐστιν and πρωτότοκος, this would seem to be the most likely conclusion.

[1] See above, pp. 3 f.

[2] Käsemann, 'Eine urchristliche Taufliturgie', *Exegetische Versuche und Besinnungen*, vol. I, p. 34. Deichgräber, p. 152, is unqualified in his agreement to this point.

[3] I have suggested it earlier in my article, 'Hymnic Elements in Ephesians 1–3', *ZNW*, vol. LVI (1965), p. 217.

[4] Gottfried Schille, *Frühchristliche Hymnen* (Berlin, 1965 (= 1962)), pp. 24 f.

14

in the arrangement given above; thus, *v.* 15*a* may also not be a part of the original. The mention of the cross is probably, as in Phil. ii. 8 and Col. i. 20, a 'Paulinism'; and the reference to 'making peace' seems to belong more closely with the references to the 'enmity'—thus raising the possibility that it is a gloss—than with the acclamatory 'He is our peace' at the beginning.

However the original may have looked exactly, the liturgical elements are also prominent here. Participial predications, *parallelismus membrorum*, and the opening αὐτός ἐστιν (cf. Col. i. 17 f.) point to the liturgical setting of this 'poem'. Whether the whole of the original is quoted here is doubtful, since the hymn sings only of reconciliation, i.e. only of that which is the theme of the second stanza of the hymn quoted in Col. i. 15–20. One may conjecture, using Col. i. 15–20 as a clue, the existence of a first stanza, also beginning with αὐτός ἐστιν, which told of the redeemer's participation in creation; but this must remain, of course, only conjecture.[1]

I TIMOTHY iii. 16

Who was manifested in the flesh,
 Was vindicated in the spirit,
Was seen by angels,
 Was proclaimed among the nations,
Was believed on in the world,
 Was taken up into glory.

The formal structure of this passage presents no problem, and the one given above is generally agreed upon (the verse is so printed in Nestle). Eduard Schweizer has pointed out that the passage is built on a chiastic structural pattern of parallelism: ab/ba/ab.[2] This makes order out of the observation that the

---

[1] Deichgräber, p. 166, rejects the notion that Eph. ii. 14–16 is a quotation of a Christological hymn, primarily on the ground that the 'both' and 'the two' are too much related to the context. But the same thing is not at all originally meant by these terms in the quotation as the context forces them to mean as they stand! Cf. below, ch. 5.

[2] Schweizer, 'πνεῦμα, πνευματικός...', *TWNT*, vol. VI, ed. Gerhard Friedrich (Stuttgart, 1959), p. 414; *idem, Erniedrigung und Erhöhung bei Jesus und seinen Nachfolgern* (Abhandlungen zur Theologie des Alten und Neuen Testaments, 28) (Zurich, 1962²), p. 105 n. 421.

terms dealing with the earthly or lower realm are in ll. 1, 4, and 5 of the passage, while those dealing with the upper or heavenly realm occur in ll. 2, 3, and 6.[1]

It is perhaps not entirely correct to refer to I Tim. iii. 16 as a hymn. In spite of the fact that the opening ὅς and the cosmic drama of which the redeemer is the subject link this passage to the others, it is lacking in certain hymnic traits. There are no participles and no *parallelismus membrorum*, only related pairs of lines. Further, although the passage seems to be complete in itself, it is far too brief and its lines too interrelated to lend itself to a division into stanzas, something which seems to characterize all the passages previously considered. Moreover, passives have not previously been encountered in these hymns in reference to the redeemer, and, except for Phil. ii. 9–11, the redeemer has always been the grammatical subject. Of course, the redeemer is *de facto* the subject here, but not grammatically so. At this passage, then, the line between 'hymn' and 'confession' seems to become blurred; if a hymn would normally exhibit confessional character, and if a confession would normally be heard in a service of worship, i.e. in the liturgy, then this blurring is certainly to be expected. Kroll had noted, with regard to I Tim. iii. 16, that 'a confession-like formula can now very probably have its place in the hymn',[2] and that this passage presents 'in content and formally a kind of symbolum'.[3] The probability, however, that the opening ὅς originally linked the passage to a preceding thanksgiving, plus the fact that I Tim. iii. 16 is praise of God in precisely the same way in which the other passages considered are praise of God, tends to justify the designation 'Christological hymn' for this passage also. It may also be that the introductory mention of the 'mystery', followed by the 'manifested' of the quotation, ties this passage to that group of passages displaying the pattern 'once hidden / now revealed' that is so closely related to

---

[1] Martin Dibelius, *Die Pastoralbriefe* (HNT 13) (Tübingen, 1955³, rev. by Hans Conzelmann), p. 50.

[2] Kroll, p. 16 n. 2.

[3] *Ibid.* p. 15. Deichgräber, p. 133, takes issue with just this statement and argues that the verse is clearly a hymn. This argument, however, is carried forward on the material rather than the formal level, i.e. I Tim. iii. 16 follows the same pattern of descent and ascent as Phil. ii. 6–11 (*ibid.* pp. 133–6). That would not prove that the verse is a hymn.

Christological statements, and hence also perhaps to liturgical materials, in the New Testament, as e.g. in Col. i. 26 f.[1] Yet I Tim. iii. 16 must be understood formally in the light of a comparison with I Pet. iii. 18–22.

I PETER iii. 18–22

In his commentary on I Peter, E. G. Selwyn declares, 'I Pet. iii. 18–22...rests in all probability on the credal hymn quoted in I Tim. iii. 16'.[2] It is of course obvious that the formula, 'Put to death in the flesh, made alive in the spirit', of I Pet. iii. 18 is comparable to the first two lines of the quotation in I Tim. iii. 16, and that the words, 'having gone into heaven', of I Pet. iii. 22 compare with the last line of the hymn in I Timothy. Selwyn goes farther, however, to see an analogy for the third line of I Tim. iii. 16, 'was seen by angels', in I Pet. iii. 19, 'having gone to the spirits in prison, he preached', and in iii. 22, 'angels and authorities and powers having been made subject to him'; and for the fourth and fifth lines, 'Proclaimed among the nations, believed on in the world', in I Pet. iii. 21, 'Baptism now saves you...an appeal to God for a good conscience'.[3] This last, however, could be considered an analogy only by inference, and Selwyn has failed to take account of the obvious parallel between ἐκηρύχθη in I Tim. iii. 16 and ἐκήρυξεν in I Pet. iii. 19. Taking these last two observations into consideration, the following original behind I Pet. iii. 18 f., 22 may be conjectured.

I Pet. iii. 18 f.	I Tim. iii. 16
18c Having been put to death in the flesh,	Was manifested in the flesh,
Having been made alive in the spirit,	Was vindicated in the spirit,
19 Having gone to the spirits in prison,	Was seen by angels,

[1] Cf. N. A. Dahl, 'Formgeschichtliche Beobachtungen zur Christusverkündigung in der Gemeindepredigt', *Neutestamentliche Studien für Rudolf Bultmann zu seinem siebzigsten Geburtstag* (BZNW, 21) (Berlin, 1954), pp. 4 f.

[2] Edward Gordon Selwyn, *The First Epistle of St Peter* (London, 1946), pp. 17 f.

[3] *Ibid.* p. 325.

He preached.[1]

Was proclaimed among
the nations,
Was believed on in the
world,

22 Who is at the right hand
of God,
Having gone into heaven,   Was taken up into glory.
Angels and authorities
and powers having been
made subject to him.

The simpler language of the Petrine passage, as compared with I Tim. iii. 16 (θανατωθείς, ζωοποιηθείς instead of ἐφανερώθη, ἐδικαιώθη; repetition of πορευθείς), the recurring participles, and the fact that the Petrine version looks more as if it were originally in two stanzas lead to the further conjecture that the original behind I Pet. iii. 18 f., 22 may have been in reality an earlier form of this hymn than that quoted in I Tim. iii. 16, instead of the reverse, as Selwyn asserted. If that should prove to be true, then one would have to assume that the author of I Timothy reduced or 'refined' the hymn into a credal statement for purposes of quotation.[2]

[1] κηρυχθείς...?

[2] The attempt of Bultmann, 'Bekenntnis- und Liedfragmente im ersten Petrusbrief', pp. 1–14, to reconstruct the original of the hymn quoted in I Pet. iii. 18–22 unfortunately failed to make full use of the parallel in I Tim. iii. 16, and it suffers from the further weakness that Bultmann found in I Pet. i. 20 an additional fragment of the same hymn. Deichgräber, pp. 169 f., evaluates positively Bultmann's conjecture that v. 20 is hymnic, but with considerable caution. A judgment more in keeping with that suggested here and by Selwyn is that of Jeremias ('Zwischen Karfreitag und Ostern', ZNW, vol. XLII (1949), pp. 195 f.). Bultmann also suggested (pp. 12 f.) that I Pet. ii. 21–4 was a hymnic passage. That we have to do here with anything other than an expanded quotation from Isa. liii is, however, unlikely. Deichgräber, pp. 140–3, concurs with Bultmann in designating I Pet. ii. 21–4 as a quotation of a hymn. The only evidence he offers, however, is to the effect that the passage is a *quotation*, because its content envisions a horizon broader than that of the context (*ibid.* p. 140 n. 5). Deichgräber also (pp. 171–3) in general rejects Bultmann's conjecture of a hymn in I Pet. iii. 18–22. It is his opinion that there is too much a mixture of prosaic and liturgical-poetic lines in these verses; but he is willing to allow *vv.* 18c and 22 to contain originally hymnic lines, although not necessarily from the same hymn. Although he is aware (*ibid.* pp. 170 f.) that

HEBREWS i. 3

Who, being the reflection of his glory and the stamp of his essence,
    Bearing everything by the word (ῥῆμα) of his power,
    Having made purification for sins,
    Sat down on the right hand of the majesty on high.

It was Günther Bornkamm who, following earlier suggestions of Ernst Lohmeyer and Ernst Käsemann, first suggested a hymnic arrangement of these lines.[1] Bornkamm suggested five lines, however, overlooking the formal parallelism between χαρακτὴρ τῆς ὑποστάσεως αὐτοῦ and ῥήματι τῆς δυνάμεως αὐτοῦ, and dividing the first line above into two lines. James Moffatt had earlier noted, however, that the metric structure of these two somewhat parallel lines provided one of the clearer examples that 'the writer [of Hebrews] was acquainted with the oratorical rhythms which were popularized by Isokrates'[2]— that is, that these lines are in meter. Thus this formal parallelism cannot be overlooked.

It seems, then, that there is present in this verse a confessional hymn of early Christianity, quite similar in some respects to the original behind I Tim. iii. 16 and I Pet. iii. 18 f., 22. One notes the opening ὅς, which likely tied the hymn originally to a preceding thanksgiving, the presence of participial predications employing substantive participles without the article, and the relation of the foregoing and following words to the other hymns being considered here. Thus the last clause of *v.* 2, 'through whom he also made the aeons', recalls Col. i. 16, as well as John i. 3 (see below); and *v.* 4, with its mention of becoming superior to the angels, is much like I Pet. iii. 22, and also recalls Phil. ii. 10.[3] These observations thus strengthen the

others have made something of the obvious relationship to I Tim. iii. 16, he seems himself not to have looked at the two passages together.

[1] Bornkamm, 'Das Bekenntnis im Hebräerbrief', *Studien zu Antike und Urchristentum*, p. 197.

[2] James Moffatt, *A Critical and Exegetical Commentary on the Epistle to the Hebrews* (ICC) (Edinburgh, 1924), p. lvi. Deichgräber, p. 139, overlooks this point and keeps to Bornkamm's arrangement.

[3] Deichgräber, p. 137, notes as especially hymnic the participial 'predications of title' in the first line.

judgment that there is present here a portion of a Christological hymn similar to the others considered. According to Bornkamm, Heb. i. 4 may in fact rely on a following part of the original, but *v.* 2 'is no more than an isolated Christ predication...', and i. 5 ff. has already dissolved too much into the theological argumentation'.[1] This judgment seems to be sound, and allows the opening ὅς of *v.* 3 to be, as the comparison with Phil. ii. 6; Col. i. 15; I Tim. iii. 16; and also Eph. ii. 14 would lead one to expect, the beginning of the hymn.

THE PROLOGUE OF THE GOSPEL OF JOHN[2]

1 In the beginning was the Word,
  And the Word was with God,
  And the Word was God.
2 He was in the beginning with God.

3 Everything was made through him,
  And apart from him was nothing made which was made.
4 In him was life,
  And the life was the light of men.

5 And the light shines in the darkness,
  And the darkness did not overcome it.

9 He was the true light,
  Which enlightens every man,
  Coming into the world.

10 He was in the world,
  And the world was made through him.
  And the world did not know him.

11 He came to his own.
  And his own did not receive him.

---

[1] Bornkamm, 'Das Bekenntnis im Hebräerbrief', pp. 198 f. Deichgräber also (p. 137) confines the hymn here to *v.* 3 and likewise (*ibid.* n. 3) leaves open the possibility that the difficult connection with *v.* 4 may imply that there was originally more to the hymn; cf. further *ibid.* p. 138.

[2] Deichgräber does not deal with this passage. He notes, however (*ibid.* p. 118 n. 3) that the prologue of the Fourth Gospel belongs among the other hymns treated here and in his work, and that he omits a discussion of the passage only 'on account of its particular problems'.

It is not entirely clear that this passage should be referred to as a 'hymn'. There are no participles in the passage, the article is generally present, and, with the exception of *v.* 3, there is no *parallelismus membrorum*; nor does the passage give evidence of being related to a thanksgiving, something which has been the case with most of the other passages considered. The obvious division into lines, however, leads one to think of poetry of some sort; and this impression is strengthened by the realization that at least two stanzas seem to be present. Thus this passage may be termed religious poetry, hence hymnic in a general sense, though perhaps not 'hymn' in the more precise sense in which the term has been used for the other passages considered.[1]

The strophic reconstruction of the original behind the prologue of John conjectured above will hardly be pleasing to everyone, so many and varied have been the attempts to reconstruct the original. The arrangement suggested here, however, in reality has much to commend it. Käsemann has already maintained that *v.* 11 is the end of the second stanza of this 'hymn', considering *v.* 12 to be a summary 'crowning of the whole'.[2] Bultmann, of course, had considered that the original quoted material extended through *v.* 16,[3] as had Rudolf Schnackenburg also.[4] Schnackenburg further deleted all of *vv.* 12 and 13 from the original, however, as being additions to the 'hymn' in the 'language of the evangelist';[5] and he was followed

---

[1] The recent attempts of Ernst Haenchen ('Probleme des johanneischen "Prologs"', *ZThK*, vol. LX (1963), pp. 305–34) and Walther Eltester ('Der Logos und sein Prophet', *Apophoreta*, pp. 109–34) to cast doubt on the hypothesis that the prologue of John is a hymn would thus to this extent be correct. Eltester's further assertion, however, that the passage is 'not praise or confession' (p. 118), that it is related to 'Christian instruction' (p. 131), relies on the thesis that *vv.* 6–8 cannot be separated stylistically from the rest of the prologue. But there is more than a stylistic difference between these verses and their context; cf. below.

[2] Ernst Käsemann, 'Aufbau und Anliegen des johanneischen Prologs', *Libertas Christiana, Festschrift für Friedrich Delekat*, ed. W. Matthias (Beiträge zur Evangelischen Theologie, 26) (Munich, 1957), p. 87.

[3] Bultmann, *Das Evangelium des Johannes* (Kritisch-exegetischer Kommentar über das NT) (Göttingen, 1959[16]), p. 53.

[4] Rudolf Schnackenburg, 'Logos-Hymnus und johanneischer Prolog', *Biblische Zeitschrift*, vol. I (1957), p. 74.

[5] *Ibid.* p. 79.

in this by Eduard Schweizer.[1] Indeed, *vv.* 12 and 13, with their mollification of the statements of *vv.* 10 and 11 that the redeemer was rejected in the world, and with their implication that redemption comes to those who believe, already depart from the sole Christological theme of the preceding material in favor of the evangelical theme of the Gospel writer. Is this not also true, however, for *vv.* 14 and 16 as well? If *vv.* 12 and 13 are the evangelist's supplementation of the passage he has quoted, *v.* 14 ('And the Word became flesh...') may be the place where the evangelist begins his Gospel with the giving of his theme.[2] *Vv.* 14 and 16, of course, must remain together. Perhaps they do reflect the existence of further material in the original, but, as was the case with Heb. i. 5 ff., the evangelist's own pen is so much in evidence here that the original can no longer be seen with any clarity.

That *vv.* 6–8, 15, and 17 f. are from the hand of the evangelist and not part of the material being quoted is reasonably clear. Not only do *vv.* 6–8 disturb the chain of 'accented words',[3] but if the original had said that John bore witness to the redeemer, it would then have to be explained why he was completely rejected in *vv.* 10 and 11.[4] There seems to be an interest on the part of the evangelist, then, in making it perfectly clear that John *only* witnessed to Christ, and *v.* 15 also fits this pattern. A similar thing is true of *v.* 17, which claims superiority for Jesus Christ over the Torah (as well as over John); and *v.* 18

[1] Schweizer, 'Aufnahme und Korrektur jüdischer Sophiatheologie im Neuen Testament', *Hören und Handeln, Festschrift für Ernst Wolf* (Munich, 1962), p. 334.

[2] This possibility was suggested by Käsemann (orally). Christoph Demke, 'Der sogenannte Logos-Hymnus im johanneischen Prolog', *ZNW*, vol. LVIII (1967), p. 61, holds *vv.* 14 and 16 to be 'the confession with which the congregation replied to the song'. Demke wishes to omit *v.* 2, however (*ibid.* pp. 52 f.), and *v.* 9 (*ibid.* p. 57) from the *Vorlage* as 'recapitulations'. Whether that is a sufficient ground is open to question.

[3] The term is Bultmann's (*Das Evangelium des Johannes*, pp. 2 f.; p. 5 n. 5), and refers to the fact that in each line of the 'hymn' there are two principal words, the second of which becomes the first principal word of the next line. This does not quite hold true for the connection between *vv.* 5 and 9, since the last 'accented word' of *v.* 5 is αὐτό and not φῶς. After this—contrary to Bultmann, who referred to the phenomenon as the 'rigid form' that held the whole passage together—the chain of 'accented words' ceases.

[4] Cf. Bultmann, *Das Evangelium des Johannes*, p. 3.

agrees completely with the theology of the evangelist in saying that only the Son has seen the Father.[1]

One is left, then, only with *vv.* 1–5 and 9–11 as having belonged, with a reasonable degree of certainty, to the original passage quoted by the evangelist at the opening of his Gospel. Both Bultmann[2] and Käsemann[3] saw a division between *vv.* 4 and 5, and Käsemann considered *v.* 5 to be the beginning of the second strophe. When one takes *v.* 11, however, to be the conclusion of the 'hymn', then one notes a certain analogy between this verse and *v.* 5. Both describe the movement of the redeemer into a realm ('darkness', 'his own') in the first line, and in the second line relate what that realm did not do to him— in both cases an aorist form of a compound of λαμβάνω. Assuming, then, as a working hypothesis, that these two lines form in either case the conclusion of a stanza, one sees that the lines prior to the concluding two lines fall in either case rather readily into two strophes—of four lines each in the first stanza, of three lines each in the second stanza.[4] The first strophe thus

[1] Cf. John v. 19 ff.; Schnackenburg, p. 74.

[2] Bultmann, *Das Evangelium des Johannes*, p. 26.

[3] Käsemann, 'Aufbau und Anliegen des johanneischen Prologs', p. 79; cf. further Schlier, 'Im Anfang war das Wort', *Die Zeit der Kirche, Gesammelte Aufsätze* (Freiburg, 1956), pp. 276 ff., and Alfred Wikenhauser, *Das Evangelium nach Johannes* (RNT, 4) (Regensburg, 1954), p. 38.

[4] If one could allow a portion of *vv.* 6–8 to stand, with H. H. Schaeder ('Der "Mensch" im Prolog des IV. Evangeliums', *Studien zum antiken Synkretismus aus Iran und Griechenland*, by Schaeder and Richard Reitzenstein (Leipzig, 1926), pp. 325 f.), who conjectured that the Aramaic original of *v.* 6 read הוא אנוש משׁור מן אלהא and is thus to be retained as referring to Enoš, who was the true subject of the original hymn, then one might be able to arrive at a strophic arrangement for the second half of the passage that would give four lines instead of three to each of the two strophes. Schaeder's hypothesis, however, is rather too speculative; and the works of E. C. Colwell (*The Greek of the Fourth Gospel* (Chicago, 1931)) and of E. Ruckstuhl (*Die literarische Einheit des Joh-Ev* (Studia Friburgensia, N.F. 3) (Freiburg in der Schweiz, 1951)) have at any rate shown that it is unnecessary to postulate a Semitic original for any portion of the Fourth Gospel in order to explain its linguistic characteristics. Schaeder's conjecture was based, of course, on the well-known work by C. F. Burney, *The Aramaic Origin of the Fourth Gospel* (Oxford, 1922), which defended the thesis 'that the Greek text of the Fourth Gospel is a translation from Aramaic' (*ibid.* p. 27). Especially Colwell's work, however, discredits this thesis considerably, in that Colwell has shown that, although the Fourth Gospel attests Aramaic idiom and syntax, similar examples can be found elsewhere in Hellenistic Greek writings.

describes the pre-existent position of the Word, the second strophe states his role as creator and as himself existing in creation as the light and life of men (whereby his role as redeemer may be implied), and the concluding two lines narrate his cosmic movement, the beginning of redemption, from the realm of light into the realm of darkness. In the next stanza, the Word successfully enters the cosmos (strophe 1), yet the cosmos does not know him (strophe 2), and when he goes to 'his own' (concluding two lines), even they do not receive him. His rejection is complete.[1]

It has perhaps become obvious by now that all these hymns and hymnic passages are materially more closely related to one another than the broad designation 'Christological' necessarily implies. Though not agreeing in detail at many points, these hymns all seem to present generally the same myth of the redeemer, involving his participation in creation, his descent and ascent to and from the world, and his work of redemption. The pattern which emerges may be represented schematically as follows:[2]

1. The redeemer possesses unity or equality with God: Phil. ii. 6; Col. i. 15 ('image of the invisible God'); Col. i. 17 ('before everything'); Heb. i. 3 ('reflection of his glory and stamp of his essence'); John i. 1 f.

2. The redeemer is mediator or agent of creation: Col. i. 16; John i. 3.

3. The redeemer is himself a part of (or is the sustainer of) creation: Col. i. 15 ('first-born of all creation'); Col. i. 17 f. ('everything is united in him, and he is the head of the body'); Heb. i. 3 ('bearing everything'); John i. 4.

---

[1] In addition to the Christological hymns discussed here, Deichgräber lists Eph. i. 20 ff. (*ibid.* pp. 161–5). Hymnic characteristics are certainly to be recognized in these verses, and the content is in keeping with the other Christological hymns. I am still unable, however, to designate with certainty enough quoted, hymnic material here to have anything to go on. Cf. my discussion in 'Hymnic Elements in Ephesians 1–3', pp. 222 f., and the whole problem there of hymn building in Ephesians. If Eph. i. 20, 22 *is* in fact a quoted hymn fragment, it in any case adds nothing to the mythological scheme given below, but rather supports it.

[2] A somewhat similar schematization of the general mythical pattern common to these passages has been given by Jacob Jervell (*Imago Dei* (Göttingen, 1960), p. 198 n. 99). Cf. further Deichgräber, p. 163.

4. The redeemer descends from the heavenly to the earthly realm: Phil. ii. 7; John i. 5, 9.

5. He dies: Phil. ii. 8; Col. i. 18 ('first-born of the dead'); I Tim. iii. 16 and I Pet. iii. 18 ('manifested in the flesh', 'put to death in the flesh').

6. He is made alive again: Col. i. 18 ('first-born of the dead'); I Tim. iii. 16 and I Pet. iii. 18 ('vindicated in the spirit', 'made alive in the spirit').

7. He effects a reconciliation: Col. i. 18 ('the beginning'); Col. i. 19 f.; Eph. ii. 14–16; I Tim. iii. 16 ('proclaimed among the nations, believed on in the world') and I Pet. iii. 19; Heb. i. 3 ('having made purification').

8. He is exalted and enthroned, and the cosmic powers become subject to him: Phil. ii. 9–11; I Tim. iii. 16 ('seen by angels, taken up into glory') and I Pet. iii. 22; Heb. i. 3 ('sat down on the right hand').

It is readily admitted that no one of the hymns includes all the acts in the mythical drama that is schematically represented here. One may recall, however, that only one of the passages, I Tim. iii. 16, is likely to be intact in its original form, and even that may be secondary; further, where one of the eight acts is not explicitly present in one of the hymns, it may be implied. For example, the line 'having made purification' in Heb. i. 3 may very well refer to the death of the redeemer (that is certainly the case for the author of Hebrews, at any rate); and the reconciliation described in Eph. ii. 14–16 and in Col. i. 18 b–20 of necessity presupposes the need for that reconciliation —therefore a fall or alienation of creation—and a descent of the redeemer to that fallen or alienated creation would probably thereby also be presupposed.

It may reasonably be assumed that this mythical drama has some background in the history of religions, that the way was already prepared in the general (or in some particular) religious milieu of early Christianity for the formulation of this particular myth—if the myth had not in reality already been formulated. The material itself thus poses the question of the definition of the background—of its characteristics and its place in the history of religions. What follows is an attempt to answer that question.

PART 2

THE CURRENT STATUS OF THE INVESTIGATION

CHAPTER 2

THE PROLOGUE OF JOHN

SOPHIA: RUDOLF BULTMANN'S EARLIER SOLUTION

Rudolf Bultmann's first attempt to explain the origin of the religious concepts in the prologue of John was his article in the Gunkel *Festschrift*.[1] Here Bultmann sought to show that the essence and function of the λόγος in the prologue of John are the same as the essence and function of the Jewish Wisdom, Sophia.

Bultmann first argued that 'the ancient *myth concerning Wisdom* is...to be seen in all clarity'. One Wisdom passage particularly to be noticed is Sir. xxiv. 1–11.[2] Here (*v.* 7) Sophia looks for a dwelling on earth and says (*v.* 8), ὁ κτίσας με κατέπαυσεν τὴν σκηνήν μου καὶ εἶπεν· ἐν Ἰακωβ κατασκήνωσον ...Also relevant is Prov. i. 20–32.[3] In this myth about Wisdom 'the pre-existent Wisdom, God's partner at the creation, seeks a dwelling place on earth among men'; but she finds no place, and her preaching goes unheeded. She comes to her own, but her own receive not. Thus she returns to the 'heavenly world' and dwells there in secret.[4] Nevertheless, as in Sap. vii.

---

[1] Bultmann, 'Der religionsgeschichtliche Hintergrund des Prologs zum Johannes-Evangelium', *Eucharisterion, Festschrift für Hermann Gunkel*, ed. Hans Schmidt, vol. II (Göttingen, 1923,) pp. 1–26.

[2] *Ibid.* p. 6.

[3]
Σοφία ἐν ἐξόδοις ὑμνεῖται,
ἐν δὲ πλατείαις παρρησίαν ἄγει,
ἐπ' ἄκρων δὲ τειχέων κηρύσσεται,
ἐπὶ δὲ πύλαις δυναστῶν παρεδρεύει,
ἐπὶ δὲ πύλαις πόλεως θαρροῦσα λέγει

.   .   .   .

διδάξω δὲ ὑμᾶς τὸν ἐμὸν λόγον.
ἐπειδὴ ἐκάλουν καὶ οὐχ ὑπηκούσατε
καὶ ἐξέτεινον λόγους καὶ οὐ προσείχετε.

[4] Bultmann, 'Der religionsgeschichtliche Hintergrund des Prologs', pp. 10 f. The view of Hans-Joachim Schoeps, *Urgemeinde–Judenchristentum–Gnosis* (Tübingen, 1956), pp. 50 f., that there is no Wisdom speculation in Prov. ix and that the hypostasis of Sophia occurs only in Kabbalistic circles of the eleventh century, is untenable, as will become increasingly obvious.

27 f.,[1] she is revealed to *some*. To the opening clause of the prologue of John, ἐν ἀρχῇ ἦν ὁ λόγος, Bultmann offered the following parallels from Wisdom literature: Prov. viii. 22–6;[2] Sir. i. 1–19;[3] xxiv. 3 f., 9;[4] and Philo *de Virtutibus* 62, πρεσβυτέραν οὐ μόνον τῆς ἐμῆς γενέσεως ἀλλὰ καὶ τῆς τοῦ κόσμου παντός.[5] Since John i. 1 seems also to be related to Gen. i. 1, Bultmann pointed out that rabbinic exegesis linked Gen. i. 1 and Prov. viii. 22 (ראשית דרכו), and cited the Jerusalem Targum on Gen. i. 1, בחוכמא ברא יי.[6] To the next clause of the prologue,

[1]   κατὰ γενεὰς εἰς ψυχὰς ὁσίας μεταβαίνουσα
      φίλους θεοῦ καὶ προφήτας κατασκευάζει.

[2]   κύριος ἔκτισέν με ἀρχὴν ὁδῶν αὐτοῦ εἰς ἔργα αὐτοῦ,
      πρὸ τοῦ αἰῶνος ἐθεμελίωσέν με ἐν ἀρχῇ,
      πρὸ τοῦ τὴν γῆν ποιῆσαι καὶ πρὸ τοῦ τὰς
                   ἀβύσσους ποιῆσαι,
      πρὸ τοῦ προελθεῖν τὰς πηγὰς τῶν ὑδάτων,
      πρὸ τοῦ ὄρη ἑδρασθῆναι,
      πρὸ δὲ πάντων βουνῶν γεννᾷ με.
      κύριος ἐποίησεν χώρας καὶ ἀοικήτους
      καὶ ἄκρα οἰκούμενα τῆς ὑπ᾿ οὐρανόν.

[3]   πᾶσα σοφία παρὰ κυρίου
      καὶ μετ᾿ αὐτοῦ ἐστιν εἰς τὸν αἰῶνα

      .   .   .   .

      προτέρα πάντων ἔκτισται σοφία
      καὶ σύνεσις φρονήσεως ἐξ αἰῶνος

      .   .   .   .

      κύριος αὐτὸς ἔκτισεν αὐτὴν
      καὶ εἶδεν καὶ ἐξηρίθμησεν αὐτὴν
      καὶ ἐξέχεεν αὐτὴν ἐπὶ πάντα τὰ ἔργα αὐτοῦ,
      μετὰ πάσης σαρκὸς κατὰ τὴν δόσιν αὐτοῦ,
      καὶ ἐχορήγησεν αὐτὴν τοῖς ἀγαπῶσιν αὐτόν.

      .   .   .   .

      καὶ εἶδεν καὶ ἐξηρίθμησεν αὐτήν,
      ἐπιστήμην καὶ γνῶσιν συνέσεως ἐξώμβρησεν
      καὶ δόξαν κρατούντων αὐτῆς ἀνύψωσεν.
      ἐγὼ ἀπὸ στόματος ὑψίστου ἐξῆλθον
      καὶ ὡς ὁμίχλη κατεκάλυψα γῆν·
      ἐγὼ ἐν ὑψηλοῖς κατεσκήνωσα,
      καὶ ὁ θρόνος μου ἐν στύλῳ νεφέλης·

      .   .   .   .

      πρὸ τοῦ αἰῶνος ἀπ᾿ ἀρχῆς ἔκτισέν με,
      καὶ ἕως αἰῶνος οὐ μὴ ἐκλίπω.

[5] Cf. also the parallels given by C. H. Dodd, *The Interpretation of the Fourth Gospel* (Cambridge, 1953), pp. 274 ff.

[6] Throughout this essay, Bultmann relied heavily on a prior essay by Hans Windisch, 'Die göttliche Weisheit der Juden und die paulinische

ὁ λόγος ἦν πρὸς τὸν θεόν, these parallels are to be noted: Sap. ix. 9;[1] viii. 3;[2] ix. 4;[3] Philo *de Ebrietate* 30 and *Legum Allegoria* ii. 49, where Sophia is the mother of the world while God is the father; and Philo *de Cherubim* 48–50 and *de Fuga et Inventione* 50. Finally, Bultmann called attention to passages in which Sophia is the creator: Prov. viii. 27–30;[4] Job xxviii. 25–7;[5]

Theologie', *Neutestamentliche Studien Georg Heinrici*, ed. Windisch (Untersuchungen zum Neuen Testament, 6) (Leipzig, 1914), pp. 220–34. Windisch had called attention in particular to the Jerusalem Targum, 'which inserts "by Wisdom" in Gen. i. 1 evidently because of the reminiscence of Prov. viii. 22' (*ibid.* p. 224). He had also noted that already in Judaism the Son of man had taken on many of the attributes of Sophia. 'The LXX first...ascribed pre-existence to the Messianic Κύριος. The Messiah in Ps. cx was originally thought of as a man who is set by God over the realm which is now to be established by God by the subduing of his enemies.' Thus Ps. cx—which is Messianic, and which refers not only to the 'subduing (reconciliation) of the enemies' (*vv.* 1 f.) but also to the 'primeval generation' (*v.* 3)—becomes the point at which Jesus, thought of in Messianic terms, can take on the attributes of Sophia (*ibid.* p. 229). The link between Messiah and Sophia is further made in the apocalyptic literature when the Son of man in I Enoch takes on attributes of Sophia. In I Enoch xlviii. 2 and 6, he, like the Sophia of Sapientia, is thought to be present at the primordial creation and to be hidden from the world (*ibid.* pp. 227 f.). Thus the concept of the Messiah is tied closely to that of Sophia in the apocalyptic literature and in the later psalms.

1 καὶ μετὰ σοῦ ἡ σοφία ἡ εἰδυῖα τὰ ἔργα σου
   καὶ παροῦσα, ὅτε ἐποίεις τὸν κόσμον.

2 εὐγένειαν δοξάζει συμβίωσιν θεοῦ ἔχουσα,
   καὶ ὁ πάντων δεσπότης ἠγάπησεν αὐτήν.

3 ...τὴν τῶν σῶν θρόνων πάρεδρον σοφίαν.

4 ἡνίκα ἡτοίμαζεν τὸν οὐρανόν, συμπαρήμην αὐτῷ,
   καὶ ὅτε ἀφώριζεν τὸν ἑαυτοῦ θρόνον ἐπ' ἀνέμων.
   ἡνίκα ἰσχυρὰ ἐποίει τὰ ἄνω νέφη,
   καὶ ὡς ἀσφαλεῖς ἐτίθει πηγὰς τῆς ὑπ' οὐρανὸν
   καὶ ἰσχυρὰ ἐποίει τὰ θεμέλια τῆς γῆς,
   ἤμην γὰρ αὐτῷ ἁρμόζουσα,
   ἐγὼ ἤμην ᾗ προσέχαιρεν.
   καθ' ἡμέραν δὲ εὐφραινόμην ἐν προσώπῳ αὐτοῦ ἐν
                                            παντὶ καιρῷ.

5 ...ἀνέμων σταθμὸν ὕδατός τε μέτρα·
   ὅτε ἐποίησεν οὕτως, ὑετὸν ἠρίθμησεν
   καὶ ὁδὸν ἐν τινάγματι φωνάς·
   τότε εἶδεν αὐτὴν [*sc.* τὴν σοφίαν, *v.* 20] καὶ
                              ἐξηγήσατο αὐτήν,
   ἑτοιμάσας ἐξιχνίασεν.

31

Prov. iii. 19;[1] Sap. ix. 1f.;[2] viii. 4;[3] vii. 12,[4] vii. 21 (ἡ πάν-των τεχνῖτις); and, 'perhaps', Prov. viii. 30.[5] The words τέκνα θεοῦ in John i. 12 are also related to Sophia, and the phrase 'has its analogy in Luke vii. 35, where the Baptist and Jesus are set forth as similar exceptions to "this generation" and are designated as children of Wisdom'.[6]

Since it is the Logos, however, who fulfills this role in the Johannine prologue, how is this change from Sophia to Logos to be explained? Bultmann answered, 'One must...suppose that either a Logos speculation existed parallel to Wisdom speculation from olden times, or that the Logos had here taken the place of the older Wisdom. The second supposition seems to me to come nearer to the truth.'[7] If this is so, then the concepts in the prologue of John are close to Alexandrian Judaism,[8] yet Bultmann thought that there was nothing *specifically* Philonic in the prologue. 'Naturally, Philo's Logos speculation belongs in the same historical religious context; it is, however, a very complicated structure.' This (Alexandrian)

[1]   ὁ θεὸς τῇ σοφίᾳ ἐθεμελίωσεν τὴν γῆν,
       ἡτοίμασεν δὲ οὐρανοὺς ἐν φρονήσει.
[2]   θεὲ πατέρων καὶ κύριε τοῦ ἐλέους
       ὁ ποιήσας τὰ πάντα ἐν λόγῳ σου
       καὶ τῇ σοφίᾳ σου κατασκευάσας ἄνθρωπον.
[3]   μύστις γάρ ἐστιν τῆς τοῦ θεοῦ ἐπιστήμης
       καὶ αἱρετὶς τῶν ἔργων αὐτοῦ.
[4]   ...αὐτῶν ἡγεῖται σοφία,
       ἠγνόουν δὲ αὐτὴν γενέτιν εἶναι τούτων.

[5] Bultmann, 'Der religionsgeschichtliche Hintergrund des Prologs', pp. 12 f.

[6] *Ibid.* p. 11.

[7] *Ibid.* p. 13. Bultmann did discuss, however, the possibility that the change went in the other direction—that is, that Sophia took over the functions of a more original Logos. That which suggests such a possibility is the Mandaean literature. Here, Enōš-Uthra is 'a (or: the) Word, a son of words', and Adamas receives the appellation 'the Word'. Also, Jōkabar is called 'the first Word' (*ibid.* p. 23).

[8] *Ibid.* p. 14. Bultmann also observed that parallels to the prologue are to be found in Babylon as well. Here, Mummu is wisdom, and Bultmann cites Damascius *de Principiis* 125: δύο δὲ ποιεῖν Ταυθὲ (Tiamat) καὶ Ἀπασῶν (Apsu), τὸν μὲν Ἀπασῶν ἄνδρα τῆς Ταυθὲ ποιοῦντες, ταύτην δὲ μητέρα θεῶν ὀνομάζοντες, ἐξ ὧν μονογενῆ παῖδα γεννηθῆναι τὸν Μωυμῖν (Mummu), αὐτὸν οἶμαι τὸν νοητὸν κόσμον ἐκ τῶν δυεῖν ἀρχῶν παραγόμενον. Also, Ea is called 'Mummu who fashions all' (Bultmann, 'Der religionsgeschicht-liche Hintergrund des Prologs', p. 21).

background will nevertheless explain how the Logos was able to take the place of the Sophia with regard to the functions mentioned. In the Hellenistic–Egyptian speculation, Bultmann explained, 'the Λόγος—in connection with old Egyptian theology and under the influence of stoic concepts—plays a special role as cosmic power. Thus it is understandable when in Alexandrian Jewish circles the Logos takes the place of the older Wisdom.' Bultmann therefore saw the replacing of Sophia with Logos in the prologue of John as presenting no more of a difficulty than the appearance of the two together in Philo.[1] There is, however, a marked difference between the Sophia of Jewish Wisdom speculation and the Logos of the Fourth Gospel. It is that, whereas Sophia appeared from time to time within or guiding different people, in John 'all light [is] concentrated on the *one* in whom the Logos became flesh'.[2] Bultmann saw the origin of the hymn of the prologue of John as lying in the identification of John the Baptist as the incarnate, Sophia-like Logos. When this concept was in turn applied to Jesus, the hymn was then correspondingly Christianized, and the anti-Baptist statements of John i. 6–8, 15 were added.

THE GNOSTIC REDEEMER: RUDOLF BULTMANN'S LATER SOLUTION

Word and Wisdom mutually dependent on an earlier tradition

Bultmann's commentary in the Meyer series provided an opportunity to answer the various critics of his earlier view as well as to incorporate into his theory of the origin of the *Vorlage*

---

[1] *Ibid.* pp. 14 f. Haenchen ('Probleme des johanneischen "Prologs"') agrees to a considerable degree with this view. Although containing several points of value in the analysis of the prologue, Haenchen's essay, however, is far too arbitrary in its discussion of the historical religious background of this passage.

[2] Bultmann, 'Der religionsgeschichtliche Hintergrund des Prologs', p. 16. Yet Bultmann nevertheless found the understanding in John i that Jesus is the Logos—an understanding which Bultmann saw as being not inherent in the *Vorlage* but brought to it by the evangelist—paralleled in Manichaeism by the affirmation that Mani is the incarnation of Wisdom (*ibid.* p. 18); cf. Reitzenstein, 'Das mandäische Buch des Herrn der Grösse und die Evangelienüberlieferung', *Sitzungsberichte der Heidelberger Akademie der Wissenschaften*, Phil.-Hist. Kl. (1919), no. 12, pp. 46 ff.

of the prologue of John changes which their observations and his own later thinking had brought about.[1]

In an excursus on 'The Logos',[2] Bultmann observes:

The evangelist could hardly begin his work with ἐν ἀρχῇ without thinking of בְּרֵאשִׁית in Gen. i. 1. And if in Gen. i God's word is not spoken of substantively, yet the creation is related back to the word of God through the 'God spoke'. Is the Λόγος thus to be understood from the *Old Testament* tradition of the word of God?[3]

Bultmann gives a negative answer to this question, since in John i the Logos is not an 'occasional event' but an 'eternal being'; the prologue speaks of the world instead of the chosen people, and of the 'Word' rather than of the word of God. Also, of course, the incarnation of *v.* 14 is not to be found in the Old Testament. Bultmann then observes that the same is also true for Judaism as for the Old Testament, 'for here also God's word did not become a "hypostasis" existing autonomously as a divine being', nor did 'word' come to be used absolutely in any other way.[4] The Wisdom, however, of the Old Testament and Judaism *will* fit, in Bultmann's opinion, the concept of the Johannine Logos.[5]

The connection, however, between Sophia and Logos can no longer be so simple as saying that Jewish Wisdom speculation is the source for the prologue of John, since Wisdom in Judaism is a synonym for Torah. Bultmann emphasizes, however, that Wisdom was not original to Judaism, but came in under foreign influence.[6] 'The Wisdom myth is...only a variant of the *revealer myth* which is propagated in Hellenistic and gnostic literature; and the relationship of the prologue of John to

---

[1] Bultmann, *Das Evangelium des Johannes* (10th to 16th edns; edns 11–16 are reprints of the 10th).

[2] *Ibid.* pp. 6–15. [3] *Ibid.* p. 6.

[4] *Ibid.* p. 7. Neither in the Greek philosophical tradition (*ibid.* p. 9) nor in Stoicism (*ibid.* pp. 9 f.) does Bultmann find the origin of the Johannine Logos. His assertion, however, that the Logos did not become a hypostasis in Judaism is simply incorrect. This will be seen in the discussion of the works of Dürr and Ringgren below.

[5] Windisch, p. 230, had called attention to the fact that according to Aristobulus, in Eusebius *Praep. Evang.* xiii. 12, 13, Sophia is the Light. Cf. Bultmann, *Das Evangelium des Johannes*, p. 8 n. 7.

[6] *Ibid.* p. 8.

Jewish Wisdom speculation is to be explained by the fact that both go back to the same tradition as their source.'[1] Bultmann now sees the relevance of Alexandrian Judaism as being an environment in which the Jewish σοφία and the Hellenistic λόγος were 'thrown together', and he sees evidence of this in Sap. ix. 1 f., where Logos and Sophia are paralleled. This 'follows the σοφία tradition, but provides the σοφία with the attributes of the λόγος'. The same observation holds true for Philo where, when Logos and Sophia concur, Sophia is 'essentially' replaced by Logos. This situation is further reflected in the *Odes of Solomon* where, 'alongside of the "word", which as a rule embodies the revelation, stands the "pure virgin" in Ode xxxiii, who is identical with the Sophia'.[2] This new interpretation of the relation of Sophia to Logos rests upon a new interpretation of the Logos: that the Logos was a gnostic figure.

Gnosticism

Bultmann describes Gnosticism as having not only a cosmogony but also an eschatology[3] in which the process of worldly creation—in which godly and anti-godly realms were combined —'must be voided by the separating of the elements'. This means that the Logos, who created the world and in so doing was dispersed in it, regains his identity (or himself) when the structure falls apart. Bultmann explains:

He is redeemed in that he redeems himself. As redeemer, the Logos himself proceeded in human form into the lower world. He clothed himself in a human body in order to deceive the demonic powers of darkness, and in order not to startle the mortals who were to be saved. Thus the concept of the incarnation of the redeemer is not

---

[1] *Ibid.* pp. 8 f. Schweizer, 'Aufnahme und Korrektur jüdischer Sophia-theologie', pp. 333 f., gives a simpler explanation of the relation of the hymn to Sophia speculation. He proposes that Christianity sought to apply concepts connected with Sophia to Jesus, and in so doing found it necessary to use a masculine designation rather than the feminine Sophia; thus the term Logos. This suggestion makes the mistake, however, of thinking that the fact that Wisdom was feminine created a problem in using Wisdom concepts to explain Jesus. That such was not the case is seen by a comparison between Luke xi. 49 and Matt. xxiii. 34.

[2] Bultmann, *Das Evangelium des Johannes*, p. 9 n. 1.

[3] *Ibid.* p. 10.

something that moved out of Christianity into Gnosticism, but is originally gnostic;[1] it was quite early taken over by Christianity and made fruitful for Christology.[2]

This gnostic redeemer idea may then enter other areas in other ways. Thus Bultmann relates Jewish Wisdom speculation, in which Sophia reveals herself in the prophets or is incarnate in the Law, to this conjectured background; and Adam speculation in 'gnosticizing, Jewish Christianity', as in the Pseudo-Clementines, is another (later) alteration of the same pattern.[3] Bultmann's characterization of the pre-Christian redeemer may well need modification; it has certainly not gone uncriticized. It nevertheless seems, since we have to do in the New Testament Christological hymns with highly similar concepts but only here with the Logos, that Bultmann has brought us a long way toward the solution of the historical religious problem when he observes, 'This figure... [is encountered] in various differentiations and *under various names*'. Some such supposition would seem

[1] This postulation of a pre-Christian gnostic redeemer myth, one of the better known ideas associated with the name of Rudolf Bultmann, has had to make its way against the older views of those who hold that the concept of a redeemer must originally have been Christian. Cf. in this regard Ernest Bevan, *Hellenism and Christianity* (London, 1921), pp. 89–108. Bevan would seem to force the evidence, however, in arguing that the *gnostic* redeemer (in such texts as the 'Hymn of the Pearl'), is only a *revealer*, whereas Gnosticism knows a *true* redeemer only where it is *Christian* Gnosticism. Regarding the Gnosticism that is Christian—that is, in which Christianity has influenced the redeemer concept, Bevan notes (*ibid.* p. 106), 'While so much in their theories can be shown to have been taken over from current paganism, no real parallel in current paganism has been discovered to the belief... of the Divine One taking upon Him for the love of men the form of a servant, coming into the sphere of darkness in order to redeem.' Of such a position, it may be said that it views the matter too simply and does not comprehend the development Bultmann has in mind. It is, however, a different matter when one of Bultmann's leading pupils, Ernst Käsemann, states, 'The pre-Christian character of the hymn is more than problematic' ('Aufbau und Anliegen des johanneischen Prologs', p. 86). Cf. also the views of Carsten Colpe (*Die religionsgeschichtliche Schule. Darstellung und Kritik ihres Bildes vom gnostischen Erlösermythus* (FRLANT, N.F. 60) (Göttingen, 1961)).

[2] Bultmann, *Das Evangelium des Johannes*, pp. 10 f. Bultmann had presented what he considered to be the clearest evidence for the existence of a pre-Christian gnostic redeemer myth in his article, 'Die Bedeutung der neuerschlossenen mandäischen und manichäischen Quellen für das Verständnis des Johannesevangeliums', *ZNW*, vol. xxiv (1925), pp. 100–46.

[3] Bultmann, *Das Evangelium des Johannes*, p. 11 n. 1.

to be necessary in order to explain why the redeemer in the prologue of John is named Logos, but apparently in Phil. ii. 6–11 Christ and in Heb. i. 3 Son. Bultmann lists as other names given to this redeemer figure δεύτερος θεός, υἱὸς θεοῦ, μονογενής, εἰκὼν τοῦ θεοῦ, δημιουργός and Ἄνθρωπος.[1]

Bultmann is not unmindful of the fact that his concept of the pre-Christian gnostic redeemer is constructed from texts that are later than the Gospel of John. He meets this difficulty squarely by holding that 'the *greater age* [of the myth] stands incontestably fast', and by emphasizing that the basic ideas are carried over into the 'religious philosophical literature of Hellenism since the first century A.D. and in[to] the Christian gnostic sources'. Ignatius, the Odes of Solomon, and the Mandaean literature are source material for this statement, and it is the fact that these writings have certain agreements, yet present variations of the same basic concepts, that 'shows that the basic concept itself reaches back into the pre-Christian period'.[2]

This statement and the one quoted above about 'various differentiations' of the figure of the gnostic redeemer seem to imply that Bultmann does not mean by the concept of a pre-Christian gnostic redeemer myth that there was at some time a particular divine being around whom this myth grew up, which myth then influenced myths about other divine beings. Rather, he seems to be saying here that, during a certain period which reaches back prior to the time of Christianity, it became common to apply certain mythological concepts to various divinities—thus there was roughly the same myth. It is not at all clear, however, that this *is* what Bultmann means, for when he speaks of the Johannine Logos and the Jewish Sophia as having a common *source*,[3] and of Adam speculation as being another *variant* of the same,[4] he seems to be referring to a particular myth for which no texts have yet been found but whose influence can nevertheless be seen in concrete instances. It may be that it was not really clear to Bultmann which of these he intended. At any rate, it would seem better to say— on the basis of Bultmann's own observations—that the several variants of the gnostic redeemer myth are precisely *not* variants

---

[1] *Ibid.* p. 11 and n. 2.   [2] *Ibid.* pp. 11 f.
[3] Above, pp. 34 f.   [4] Above, p. 36.

of a single myth, but are the products of similar backgrounds, of a common religious environment. Thus it would not be a question of one figure's influencing others, but rather of the concurrent development of several similar figures within a particular religious environment, e.g. Hellenistic Judaism. If such could be shown to be the case, then there would still quite probably have been mutual influence among them; but this is a different matter altogether from saying that the concept of one redeemer *figure* influenced the concepts of other divine beings.

Early oriental Gnosticism

Bultmann defines the particular type of Gnosticism that lies behind the prologue of John as early oriental—which is to be distinguished from the Syrian–Egyptian type[1]—similar to that found in the Odes of Solomon. He finds this classification supported when traces of the 'Iranian' type are encountered elsewhere in the Gospel (viii. 44; xii. 31; xiv. 30; xvi. 11),[2] in which the darkness stands diametrically opposed to God. Yet, with regard to the Logos of John i, Bultmann refers to the 'peculiar duality of the historical situation'. Whereas the earlier gnostic view of a 'manifoldness of the divine Being, of Pleroma and Aeons', normally in Gnosticism later becomes a 'speculative doctrine of the gradual unfolding of Being', this transition has not taken place in the Odes of Solomon, Ignatius, the monotheistic Mandaean writings, and the source of the prologue of John; but rather the *earlier* idea is present in this literature.[3] That western as well as later oriental gnostic systems fail in their attempt to make 'the proceeding of the Logos from the Father' understandable is further evidence that we have to do here with early oriental Gnosticism. The other side of the 'peculiar duality' is then seen in the fact that the myth here and in the Odes of Solomon is 'developed', i.e. 'reduced', and that the λόγος has lost its relation to language in the prologue of John. Evidence of a more primitive Gnosticism, in which the λόγος was still thought of as spoken 'word', may yet be seen in the

---

[1] Cf. Hans Jonas, *The Gnostic Religion* (Boston, 1958), pp. 101–237, particularly pp. 236 f.

[2] Bultmann, *Das Evangelium des Johannes*, p. 13 and n. 5.

[3] *Ibid.* p. 13 and nn. 7, 8.

Odes of Solomon. Ode xii, particularly *v.* 8; Ode viii, where the Logos himself speaks; and Ode.xlii. 6, where he speaks through others, are particularly to be noted.[1]

Bultmann makes one further observation with regard to the Gnosticism of the prologue of John. As in Jewish Wisdom literature, the Odes of Solomon, and the 'Hymn of the Pearl',[2] the origin of the world and of man in the prologue of John is not a tragedy. This fact distinguishes this body of literature from the rest of Gnosticism, and is also to be explained by the influence of the Old Testament. Bultmann summarizes:

> It follows therefore that the source of the prologue belongs within the circle of a relatively early Gnosticism, which has been expanded under the Old Testament belief in God as the creator. This has occurred in such a way that the mythology is strongly repressed, that the gnostic cosmology is dislodged in favor of belief in the creation, and that interest in the relation of man to the revelation of God, thus the soteriological interest, has become primary.[3]

This supposition of a 'reduction' of gnostic mythology is probably the least satisfactory part of Bultmann's explanation and raises the possibility that his conjecture of a pre-Christian gnostic redeemer myth is to this extent incorrect. The conjecture can hardly be entirely incorrect, however, since a common myth seems to be presupposed by the several New Testament Christological hymns.

JUDAISM: C. H. DODD

The major alternative to Bultmann for Johannine interpretation in the generation just drawing to a close is of course C. H. Dodd. In his important work on the Fourth Gospel,[4] Dodd offers a thorough examination of other bodies of literature related in thought to the Fourth Gospel (*Corpus Hermeticum*, Mandaean literature, Gnosticism), yet considers the conceptuality of the Fourth Gospel to represent an independent development. Particularly regarding Gnosticism, Dodd asserts that 'there is

[1] *Ibid.* p. 14 n. 1. Cf. the other literature referred to there.
[2] *Acta Thomae* cviii–cxiii.
[3] Bultmann, *Das Evangelium des Johannes*, pp. 14 f.
[4] Dodd, *The Interpretation of the Fourth Gospel.*

no Gnostic document known to us which can with any show of probability be dated...before the period of the New Testament'; and he labels attempts to demonstrate the pre-Christian origin of Gnosticism as 'speculative'.[1] He further notes the parallels between the Logos of the prologue of John and what he terms 'Gnostic mediators' in the various gnostic systems, yet he dismisses the possibility of any close connection by noting that the mediator is normally not called Logos[2]—an argument that is without value when one realizes the possibility, as Bultmann did,[3] that the gnostic mediator or redeemer is precisely variously named in the various bodies of literature.

Dodd finally explains the origin of the Logos in the prologue of John as being Judaism, normative Judaism with some ideas from the Wisdom literature and from Philo brought in.[4] Dodd concludes that

the ambiguity which (from our point of view) enters into the Johannine conception of the Logos could be understood if we assumed that the author started from the Jewish idea of the Torah as being at once the Word of God and the divine Wisdom manifested in creation, and found, under the guidance of Hellenistic Jewish thought similar to that of Philo, an appropriate Greek expression which fittingly combined both ideas.[5]

Although Dodd's emphasis that the gnostic literature of the Christian era seems to be only little affected by Christian literature is doubtless correct (in this he does not disagree with Bultmann), he seems to have failed to see the consequences of this observation. Dodd would hold that the known gnostic literature has its place within a development; thus, there must have been prior stages of the development and presumably even prior literature. Yet, if there are no sources showing a gnostic background for parts of the New Testament, then there are no sources showing a gnostic background for Gnosticism. When, therefore, ideas more or less related to ideas found in gnostic literature appear in the New Testament, it would seem more logical to assume that their appearance there is related to the

[1] *Ibid.* p. 98.   [2] *Ibid.* p. 109.   [3] Above, p. 37.
[4] *Ibid.* pp. 268–78. Cf. particularly p. 270: What is said of the Logos in John i. 1–18 is 'in harmony with the general thought of Judaism'.
[5] *Ibid.* p. 278.

development of Gnosticism than to assume that it is not. To insist that gnostic-*like* ideas, when they occur in the New Testament, are unrelated to the development of Gnosticism may even be unrealistic, since that would mean that the concepts found in the New Testament that are closest to its broad Hellenistic environment came into existence without the influence of that environment. In addition, it appears somewhat artificial when Dodd postulates a composite Jewish background for the Logos of the prologue of John, ideas from which were molded into a unified whole by the author of the Gospel. It is one thing when a writer employs an existing thought motif—in this case a myth—to clarify or explain a new event. In such a case, the motif is filled with new meaning, and the understanding of the event is shifted in the direction of the previous understanding of the myth. It is something else, however, when a writer consciously pulls together strands from different (though related) traditions to create a whole that is greater than the sum of its parts, or that is at least quite different from any of the parts. That New Testament writers employed existing concepts (Messiah, Kyrios, to name only two of the more prominent) to explain the Christ event is well known; but an example for the kind of seemingly artificial construction suggested by Dodd for the prologue of John seems to be lacking in the New Testament.

Thus it should be clear that the myth found in the New Testament Christological hymns has a background, indeed a specific background, and that one may inquire further after this background.

INTRA-CHRISTIAN ORIGIN: RUDOLF SCHNACKENBURG

To some, Bultmann's suggestion that Alexandrian Sophia speculation lay in some way behind the prologue of John seemed to endanger the prologue by making it 'heretical'. One way in which Bultmann was countered at this point was in the demonstration that the prologue was not dissimilar from the remainder of the Gospel in vocabulary, idiom, and usage. Thus, to the extent that the bulk of the material in the Gospel was not suspect of the same background, the prologue could be returned

THE CURRENT STATUS OF THE INVESTIGATION

to the fold of that which was originally and authentically Christian.[1] To show this stylistic relation of the prologue to the rest of the Gospel was the work of Ruckstuhl.[2] We need do no more than refer to his work here and call attention to the fact that he has fairly convincingly linked to parallel passages in the Gospel most of the passages in the prologue on which Bultmann leaned so heavily for his parallels with Wisdom literature, such as e.g. *vv.* 2, 5, 12, 14*b*, and *c*.[3]

Accepting the validity of Ruckstuhl's work—though not its conclusion, that the prologue is the work of the author of the Gospel—Rudolf Schnackenburg attempted to speak further to the problem of the religious background of the prologue by focusing attention upon those elements which Ruckstuhl had *not* been able to associate with the rest of the Gospel.[4] The use of the absolute ὁ λόγος Schnackenburg considered to be Hellenistic, in contrast to the 'Word of God' in Rev. xix. 13, which he defined as 'Old Testament-biblical'; and the idea that the incarnate Logos enlightens every man he also saw as unJohannine. Since Ruckstuhl had shown *vv.* 14*b* and *c* to be in the style of the rest of the Gospel, 14*a* and *d* must then belong to the original hymn, thus: 'And the Logos became flesh and camped among us...full of grace and truth.'[5] Thus the hymn has for Schnackenburg an *anti*-gnostic tendency:

Bultmann does not dispute that, but he gives to the celebrated expression καὶ ὁ λόγος σάρξ ἐγένετο a meaning which draws out of the expression, in a peculiar manner, both gnostic and anti-gnostic

---

[1] Whether indeed any religious language or religious objectifications of self-understanding contained in the New Testament are originally and authentically Christian is a problem with which we cannot deal here.

[2] Ruckstuhl, *Die literarische Einheit*. This was of course also a consistent assumption of Burney. Burney obviously considered the evidence presented throughout the discussion of the prologue (*ibid.* pp. 28–43) to confirm the assumption; cf. particularly *ibid.* p. 39. E. C. Colwell seems also, from a completely different point of view, to have raised the possibility of unity by showing that the language of the prologue is acceptable Greek.

[3] Cf. also T. Evan Pollard, 'Cosmology and the Prologue of the Fourth Gospel', *VChr*, vol. xii (1958), p. 149, who sees the prologue as written by the author of the Gospel 'as a summary of the *Heilsgeschichte* of which the incarnate life of the Son of God is the central point'.

[4] Schnackenburg, 'Logos-Hymnus und johanneischer Prolog'.

[5] *Ibid.* pp. 76–9.

elements. He sees the evangelist as having appropriated for himself the mythological language of Gnosticism, but the particular formulation 'the Logos became flesh' as revealing the stumbling block of the revelation.[1]

Schnackenburg thought he had improved on this view by supposing that the 'Logos hymn stemmed from the very beginning from Christian circles'. These circles were not acquainted with the concept of a mythical redeemer who came to earth, but only with 'the eternal, only Son of God, who at one time became man—a real, flesh and blood man—in the person of Jesus of Nazareth'.[2]

Such an alternative does not, however, seem to be tenable, since it relies so heavily on the originality of *v.* 14*a*,[3] whereas it has been seen in ch. 1 that there is some question on formal grounds whether anything after *v.* 11 belongs with the original hymn. There is also, however, a problem of a material nature with Schnackenburg's solution; for when he defines the Christian community from which this hymn must have come, it is one that 'came into conversation with Jewish and heathen Hellenism'.[4] To insist, then, that the hymn is of Christian origin does not solve the problem but only obscures it, for it makes little difference whether one has to do here with a pre-Christian hymn adapted for Christian use, or with a Christian hymn that made use of pre-Christian ('Jewish and heathen Hellenistic') concepts. It is the question of the origin of these concepts which Schnackenburg has left unanswered.

LOGOS: LORENZ DÜRR

The Word in hymnic material

Although Bultmann considered the *Vorlage* of the prologue to be a song,[5] he made no use of this observation for his inquiry into the religious background of the prologue. It remained for Lorenz Dürr, working evidently entirely independently of Bultmann (as Bultmann was of him), to apply the formal observation that the *Vorlage* was a hymn to the problem of

---

[1] *Ibid.* p. 94. [2] *Ibid.* pp. 94 f.
[3] Cf. also *ibid.* pp. 96 f. [4] *Ibid.* p. 97.
[5] Bultmann, *Das Evangelium des Johannes*, p. 5.

religious backgrounds. In his work,[1] Dürr first called attention to what he defined materially as 'descriptions of majesty' and formally as 'berākhōth'.[2] When he cites, however, Ps. xcii. 2–4 (הַלְלוּיָהּ...כִּי); cxlvii. 1 (טוֹב לְהוֹדוֹת לַיֹּי); lxv. 2 (לְךָ דֻמִיָּה תְהִלָּה); Ps. Sol. xv. 2–3 (ἐξομολογήσασθαί σοι ἐν ἀληθείᾳ); (נָעִים נָאוָה תְהִלָּה); and Ode Sol. xvi. 1 ff. (ܐܝܟ ܣܘܢ ܪܚܡܐ ܕܝܢ ... ܕܗܘܝܘܬ, My work is the psalm of the Lord in his praises),[3] one sees that his *Gattung* is poorly named. These passages, with many others that begin similarly, were designated simply 'hymns' by Gunkel,[4] and this designation would still seem to be more appropriate, as the discussion on pp. 1–5 showed. The term *berachah* should be used only in reference to a formula used in Jewish prayers and hymns beginning with בָּרוּךְ יי :ברך, בָּרוּךְ אַתָּה אֱלֹהֵינוּ, or something similar. When Dürr claims, however, that among these hymns, which are not limited only to Palestine and Syria, 'hymns to the "Word of the Godhead" (Sumerian *enem*, Accadian *amâtu*) share first place',[5] this is certainly enough to awaken our interest.[6]

Dürr first examines the Word in Sumerian and Babylonian hymns. In these 'Word hymns' there is 'a series of beneficent actions...which do not at all fit into the category of voice, thunder; here *enem* most definitely has the meaning of "*epiš pika*" or "*ṣit pîšu*" of the [cuneiform] texts, i.e. the *objective*,

---

[1] Lorenz Dürr, *Die Wertung des göttlichen Wortes im Alten Testament und im Antiken Orient* (Mitteilungen der vorderasiatisch-aegyptischen Gesellschaft, XLII. Band, 1. Heft) (Leipzig, 1938). The location of this work apparently explains the lack of attention it has received from biblical scholars.

[2] *Ibid.* p. 3.

[3] The numbering of the Odes of Solomon throughout this work is that of Walter Bauer (ed.), *Die Oden Salomos* (Kleine Texte für Vorlesungen und Übungen, 64) (Berlin, 1933). This was adopted because Bauer's was the only edition presenting the Syriac in *parallelismus membrorum*. Since, however, an English translation already exists (*The Odes and Psalms of Solomon*, vol. II, trans. with introduction and notes by Rendel Harris and Alphonse Mingana (Manchester, 1920)), this translation is used, except when reference to the Syriac necessitates a change. In such cases, the material is enclosed in parentheses.

[4] Gunkel, 'Psalmen', cols. 1613 f.   [5] Dürr, p. 3.

[6] The formal relation of Jewish liturgy to that of Babylon was indicated by Norden, p. 207. He wrote: 'It is...conceivable that the Jewish prayer ritual, at least in its formal garb, presents itself as the last offshoot of the old Babylonian.' Cf. further *ibid.* pp. 214–20.

divine Word that acts in the world and passes through the world'.[1] One can thus speak of '*unum dúg-ga zida*', 'Lord of the lawful Word'.[2] There is lacking in Babylon and Assyria, however, 'a cosmogony in the sense of the creation by the divine Word';[3] but there *is* present in Assyria, albeit only in Assyria, the concept that God's Word is 'the exalted, powerful [Word]... thus also *unfathomable* and *incomprehensible, closed up, mysterious*'.[4]

In Egypt, one finds what one might already have expected from Bultmann's earlier work,[5] that the Word is associated with wisdom. Here Thoth, the Egyptian Hermes and also the god of wisdom, is esteemed as the Word.[6] '...Thoth, the great, who has created all things, the tongue and the heart, which knows all things...' is part of a text from a temple wall at Dendera. It is even said of him, 'All that is has come into being through his word.'[7]

The hypostatization of the Word in Israel

In spite of some similarities to the Egyptian situation, the hypostatization of the Word in Israel shows primarily eastern influence. The concept expressed by the Accadian *ṣit pîšu* (= 'the going forth from his [the] mouth [of the godhead]' or 'the breath of the [divine] mouth') is also to be found in the Old Testament, as is seen by the parallelism of Spirit, Breath, with the Word (דָּבָר) in Ps. xxxiii. 6; cxlvii. 18; and Deut. viii. 3.[8] The process of the hypostatization of the Word in the Old

---

[1] Dürr, p. 6.   [2] *Ibid.* p. 8.   [3] *Ibid.* p. 32.   [4] *Ibid.* pp. 60 f.

[5] That Bultmann moved the origin of the Johannine Logos from Alexandria to Trans-Jordan in his commentary was not because he no longer thought it was related to Alexandrian Wisdom speculation, but because he had decided that both ideas had their origin in oriental Gnosticism.

[6] Cf. Reitzenstein, *Zwei religionsgeschichtliche Fragen nach ungedruckten griechischen Texten der Strassburger Bibliothek* (Strassburg, 1901), p. 73, who saw the early designation of Thoth as the messenger, i.e. word of Re as being the origin of the hypostatization of the Word.

[7] *De Rochem.*, Edfu I 289; Zeit des Ptolemäus IV; *De Rochem.* II 16, quoted in Dürr, p. 28.

[8] *Ibid.* p. 21. P. Georg Ziener, *Die theologische Begriffssprache im Buche der Weisheit* (Bonner biblische Beiträge, 11) (Bonn, 1956), pp. 142 f., points out that the πνεῦμα of Sapientia can take on qualities one would expect to be attributed there to Sophia. Thus with Sap. i. 7, where the spirit πεπλήρωκεν τὴν οἰκουμένην and is τὸ συνέχον τὰ πάντα, is to be compared viii. 1, where Sophia διοικεῖ τὰ πάντα.

Testament then proceeds in this manner:[1] From a mere *sermo operatorius* in Ps. xxxiii. 9; cxlviii. 5; and Judith xvi. 15, the Word can become a medium of God's action.

Ps. xxxiii. 6:

By the word of the Lord the heavens were made,
and all their host by the breath of his mouth.

The next step in the process is for the Word to become 'an absolutely divine show of force'. Thus Sir. xxxix. 17*b*:

At his word (λόγος) the waters stood in a heap,
and the reservoirs of water at the word (ῥῆμα) of his mouth;

or Sap. ix. 1 f.:

God...

Who hast made all things by thy word,
and by thy wisdom hast formed man.[2]

In IV Ezr. vi. 38 ff. the Logos assumes still more explicit powers of creation, is thus further hypostatized: 'And I said: O Lord, of a truth thou didst speak at the beginning of the creation upon the first day, saying: Let heaven and earth be made! And thy word perfected the work...as soon as thy word went forth the work was done' (translation mine).

Coincident with this hypostatizing process, there comes in the idea of the Word as savior,[3] as in Ps. cvii. 20:

He sent forth his word, and healed them,
and delivered them from destruction;

and Sap. xvi. 12, where the concept of the word is proceeding farther in the direction of autonomy from God:

For neither herb nor poultice cured them,
but it was thy word, O Lord, which heals all men.

Similarly, there is the growth of the idea of the Word as a word of power. Thus when Isa. xi. 4 says, וְהִכָּה־אֶרֶץ בְּשֵׁבֶט פִּיו, 'and he shall smite the earth with the rod of his mouth', the Messiah's word is thought of as having power; but it is a considerable step beyond this in the direction of hypostatization when

---

[1] Dürr, pp. 38–40.

[2] If the progress from step 2 to step 3 is not clear here, neither is it helped when one examines the sources, for where the Hebrew in Ps. xxxiii. 6 is בִּדְבַר, the Greek of Sap. ix. 1 is ἐν λόγῳ. Thus Dürr seems to be making a distinction at this point where there is none. He is correct, however, in seeing an advance in hypostatization here over the earlier *sermo operatorius*.

[3] *Ibid.* p. 45.

Sap. xviii. 15 refers to ὁ παντοδύναμός σου λόγος. When one then finds in Heb. i. 3 this predication of the redeemer, φέρων τε τὰ πάντα τῷ ῥήματι τῆς δυνάμεως αὐτοῦ;[1] or in Heb. iv. 12, 'For the word of God is living and active, sharper than any two-edged sword, piercing to the division of soul and spirit, of joints and marrow, and discerning the thoughts and intentions of the heart'[2] (RSV), Dürr calls this a full hypostatization.[3] Still again, the Word receives the power of destruction, Sap. xii. 9:

ἢ θηρίοις δεινοῖς ἢ λόγῳ ἀποτόμῳ ὑφ' ἓν ἐκτρῖψαι

or to destroy them at one blow by dread wild beasts
or thy stern word.

'All the same, the Word is clearly no longer thought of as a mere living power...but already as a quantity (hypostasis) which emanates from [God] and which not only has become autonomous but acts autonomously.' This autonomous Word can also be a sustaining force or being. Thus a primitive stage of the development is preserved in Sir. xliii. 10:

At the command of the Holy One (ἐν λόγοις ἁγίου)

they [sc. the stars] stand as ordered;

whereas this same concept appears in conjunction with a Logos more fully hypostatized in Sap. xvi. 26:

Thy word preserves those who trust in thee.[4]

Once again, Dürr points out that this concept of a word that can act in the world without proceeding from the mouth of

---

[1] Here then is a further insight into the material relationship between this hymnic passage and the hymn of John i. It will be remembered that the Logos in John i is paradoxically made, though he is the redeemer, equal to, the same as, God: θεὸς ἦν ὁ λόγος (cf. Bultmann, *Das Evangelium des Johannes*, p. 17). Thus, since he is both God and God's Word, it could almost be said that τὰ πάντα came into being through the word of the Logos. This would be a linguistic but not a speculative absurdity. What has happened in Heb. i. 3, then, is that the redeemer referred to by the opening ὅς has, with regard to τὰ πάντα, actually taken the place of the God of John i. 3, and the ῥῆμα of Heb. i. 3 is thus parallel to the λόγος of John i. 3 (ῥῆμα and λόγος both render the Aramaic מֶלְּא; cf. Dan. ii. 9). This connection has also been seen by Roy A. Stewart ('Creation and Matter in the Epistle to the Hebrews', *NTS*, vol. XII (1966), p. 289), who notes that Philo juxtaposes the two terms in *Leg. Alleg.* iii. 131 and in *de Posteritate Caini* 102.

[2] Ζῶν γὰρ ὁ λόγος τοῦ θεοῦ καὶ ἐνεργὴς καὶ τομώτερος ὑπὲρ πᾶσαν μάχαιραν δίστομον καὶ διϊκνούμενος ἄχρι μερισμοῦ ψυχῆς καὶ πνεύματος, ἁρμῶν τε κα' μυελῶν, καὶ κριτικὸς ἐνθυμήσεων καὶ ἐννοιῶν καρδίας.

[3] Dürr, p. 62 f.　　　　　[4] *Ibid.* pp. 45-7.

God has been found 'mostly...in hymns and prayers'.[1] It is particularly important, then, when the Word in this hymnic literature is associated with Truth and Light.

Ps. cxix. 160:

רֹאשׁ־דְּבָרְךָ אֱמֶת (Gr.: ἀρχὴ τοῦ λόγου[2] σου ἀλήθεια), the beginning of thy word is truth (translation mine);

Dan. x. 1: אֱמֶת הַדָּבָר, the word is truth (translation mine);

Ps. cxix. 105:

נֵר־לְרַגְלִי דְבָרֶךָ וְאוֹר לִנְתִיבָתִי, LXX: Λύχνος τοῖς ποσίν μου ὁ λόγος σου καὶ φῶς ταῖς τρίβοις μου, thy word is a lamp unto my foot and a light unto my path (translation mine).[3]

Word and Wisdom

Finally, Dürr calls attention to the fact that the changes in the concept of the Word in the Old Testament and Judaism are parallel to the changes in the concept of Wisdom. Thus, when in Isa. lv. 10 f.[4] the Word goes out, will not return empty, and does what God wishes, a parallel is provided for Prov. viii, where Sophia is thought of as somewhat autonomous, but not yet a full hypostasis.[5] When, then, in Sap. xviii. 14–16 one reads:

For while gentle silence enveloped all things,
and night in its swift course was now half gone,
thy all-powerful word leaped from heaven, from the royal throne,
into the midst of the land that was doomed,
a stern warrior carrying the sharp sword of thy authentic command,
and stood and filled all things with death,
and touched heaven while standing on the earth,

---

[1] *Ibid.* p. 51.   [2] LXX and Hieronymus: τῶν λόγων.

[3] Dürr, pp. 73–5.

[4]   For as the rain and the snow come down from heaven,
            and return not thither but water the earth,
        making it bring forth and sprout,
            giving seed to the sower and bread to the eater,
        so shall my word be that goes forth from my mouth;
            it shall not return to me empty,
        but it shall accomplish that which I purpose,
            and prosper in the thing for which I sent it.

[5] Dürr, p. 123.

48

one sees that there is present a concept parallel to the Sophia of this work.[1] The difference between Deutero-Isaiah and Sapientia is that the Word in the latter is an autonomous power. 'From here, however, it is only a step to a hypostasis in the specifically historical religious sense.'[2]

The hymn in John i, then, is seen by Dürr as the end result of the process of hypostatization that has moved from Gen. i to Sap. xviii,[3] and he sees the author of the Gospel as influenced not by the figure of Hermes/Logos or the stoic Logos, but rather as using an idea growing naturally out of the Old Testament and Jewish wisdom literature.[4] 'He himself took up the Logos concept because he could in this way best express the essence and activity of his Christ, the Son of God.'[5] In this, Dürr does not seem to be aware that it is only in the hymn used in his prologue that the evangelist speaks in this sense of the Logos, and that the hymn is therefore to be seen as an independent unit apart from the rest of the Gospel. Also, his conclusion that the Logos of John i is to be explained *merely* from the background of Jewish Logos speculation does not go as far toward explaining the revealer/redeemer aspect of the Johannine Logos as Bultmann's explanation from the hypothesis of the gnostic redeemer myth. Nevertheless, Dürr's study seems to have provided a necessary supplement to Bultmann's. Dürr has given evidence that *there was in pre-Christian Judaism a concept of a divine Logos who could come to earth to do God's will and return again to heaven*, and who, if Sophia was one, was at least a forerunner of another 'variant of the *revealer myth* which was expanded in

[1] Other passages showing the same stage of hypostatization are Ps. cvii. 20; cxlvii. 15; and Sap. xvi. 12 and 26 (*ibid.* pp. 125 ff.).

[2] This same development was also traced, much more briefly, by Jules Lebreton, *History of the Dogma of the Trinity from its Origins to the Council of Nicea*, vol. i, trans. Algar Thorold (London, 1939), pp. 98–100.

[3] Dürr, pp. 158 ff.

[4] Dodd, p. 265, suggests that the general concept of a hypostasis was 'extremely widespread', but that the supposition that the use of λόγος in this way was 'very widely current' is not to be made. In this, he does not seem to be aware of the evidence presented here by Dürr. This oversight was also noted by W. F. Albright, 'Recent Discoveries in Palestine and the Gospel of John', *The Background of the New Testament and its Eschatology, in Honour of Charles Harold Dodd*, edd. W. D. Davies and D. Daube (Cambridge, 1954), p. 169 n. 4.

[5] Dürr, pp. 166 f.

Hellenistic and gnostic literature'.[1] That this Logos is, more than Sophia, specifically connected with 'hymns and prayers' seems to make him much closer to the prologue of John than is Sophia.

THE PROCESS OF HYPOSTATIZATION:
HELMER RINGGREN

The general environment with regard to hypostatization

If Dürr attempted to explain the origin of the Logos in John as the end product of a process of hypostatization within Judaism, and in so doing complemented Bultmann's explanation of the religious origin of this Logos by showing that the Word was parallel to rather than dependent on Wisdom in the Jewish tradition—whatever might have been the factors influencing the development of these two figures—it was Helmer Ringgren who, using Dürr's work fairly extensively in places, placed this process of hypostatization in its larger context.[2] Ringgren's work, which is a study of hypostatization in all its aspects in the ancient world generally, begins with Egypt, where there were two deities named Hu and Sia (*ḥw* and *sjȝ*), which mean respectively 'word, command', and 'intelligence, understanding'.[3] These beings are honored, at an early date, as having assisted in creation,[4] and Hu is particularly the mediator of creation. 'Nothing has come into existence that he has not said (=without his word).'[5] Other hypostases in Egypt were Hike (*ḥkȝ*), Magic,[6] Seeing and Hearing (*mȝȝ* and *śḏm*),[7] and Maat (*mȝʿ.t*, Coptic με, μηι, μεε), Truth.[8] Also to be noted

---

[1] Bultmann, *Das Evangelium des Johannes*, p. 9.

[2] Helmer Ringgren, *Word and Wisdom. Studies in the Hypostatization of Divine Qualities and Functions in the Ancient Near East* (Lund, 1947).

[3] *Ibid.* p. 9. Here should be noted the attempt of Reitzenstein, *Zwei religionsgeschichtliche Fragen*, to derive the Logos of the Johannine prologue from Egyptian speculation. One could refer to the Egyptian Hermes, i.e. Thoth as the being δι' οὗ οἰκονομήθη τὸ πᾶν (*ibid.* p. 58). This Hermes, who, because of his function as ἑρμηνεύς, could also be called Logos, must then have influenced Philo, who designates Moses as the ἑρμηνεὺς νόμων, i.e. Logos. Reitzenstein thus understood John i. 17 as being the assertion of the evangelist that Jesus, not Moses, is the proper Logos (*ibid.* pp. 102 f.).

[4] Ringgren, p. 12.

[5] É. Chassinat, *Le temple de Dendara*. 1–4, III (Cairo, 1934–5), p. 137, quoted in Ringgren, p. 13.   [6] Ringgren, p. 27.

[7] *Ibid.* p. 37.   [8] *Ibid.* p. 45.

are the fourteen Kas of Re: Word, Abundance, Glory, Service, Making, Magic, Prosperity, Sparkle, Victory, Strength, Brightness, Brilliance, Honor, and Preparedness.[1] Of Maat, Ringgren says:

We have evidence for Maat as a goddess in the Pyramid texts, and there are numerous examples of priests and prophets of Maat as early as the Old Kingdom. A temple of Maat is known from the Middle Kingdom, and from the New Kingdom there are several instances of such temples. A goddess playing such a part in the cult, may—it is true—be originally an 'abstraction' or a hypostatized function, but she is not to religious thought 'an artificial product'. She is a goddess like other goddesses.[2]

Ancient Sumer and Akkad are almost equally as rich in hypostatized beings. There are, 'in the suite of the goddess Damkina,...two messengers or ministers called Uznu, "ear, understanding", and Ḥasīsu, "wisdom"'.[3] Since Damkina is the lady of the god Ea, 'and as Ea is the god of wisdom,[4] it is quite natural to find Understanding and Wisdom in his court'. There is also Tašmētu, hearing or mercy. The process of hypostatization did not always go so far, however, as to result in the creation of independent deities, and Ringgren notes that there are also cases of 'what I should like to call hypostases in the making'.[5]

Hypostatization in Canaan and Israel: the primacy of Wisdom

From Egypt and Assyria/Babylonia, Ringgren moves closer to Israel. Here he finds hypostases in the Ras-Shamra texts:

RS 4474:

'il bn 'il	El, sons of El [i.e. gods],
dr bn 'il	generation of sons of El,
mpḫrt bn 'il	Assembly of sons of El,
ṯrmn wšnm	Ṯrmn and Šnm,
'il w'atrt	El and Atirat,
ḥnn 'il	grace of El,
nṣbt 'il	firmness [?] of El,

---

[1] *Ibid.* p. 39.   [2] *Ibid.* p. 52.   [3] *Ibid.* p. 59.
[4] He is called *ilEa bēl uzni ḫasīsi*, lord of Understanding and Wisdom (*ibid.*).
[5] Ringgren, p. 63.

šlm 'il	peace of El,
'il ḫš il 'add	—
b'd ṣpn 'd/l ugrt	by the 'd of Ṣapan, by the 'd of Ugarit,
bmrh 'il	by the delight of El,
bn'it 'il	by the grace of El,
bṣmd 'il	by the suite of El,
bdṯn 'il	by the dṯn of El,
bšrp 'il	by the šrp [burnt offering?] of El,
bknt 'il	by the laws [?or: truth] of El,
bgdyn 'il	by the gdyn of El.[1]

Here, though it is not hypostatized, wisdom is connected with El and his word:

II AB IV, 41 f.:

tḥmk 'il ḥkm	Thy word, o El, is wisdom
ḥkmt 'm 'lm	wise art thou eternally.

V AB E, 38 f.:

tḥmk 'il ḥkm	Thy word, o El, is wisdom
ḥkmk 'm 'lm	thy wisdom is everlasting.[2]

In Job xv. 7[3] an interesting thing occurs with regard to Wisdom:

[1] *Ibid.* pp. 74 f.

[2] *Ibid.* pp. 79 f. It should be noted how easily, by the change of a single consonant, this text could be altered so that Wisdom is started on the path to autonomy. W. F. Albright, 'Some Canaanite–Phoenician Sources of Hebrew Wisdom', *Wisdom in Israel and in the Ancient Near East. Festschrift for H. H. Rowley*, edd. Martin Noth and D. Winton Thomas (Supplements to *Vetus Testamentum*, 3) (Leiden, 1955), pp. 7 f., interprets this passage and others as meaning that the origin of the figure of Sophia in the Old Testament and Judaism is 'older Canaanite mythological imagery'. That parallels with the Jewish Sophia are found in the indigenous Canaanite religion is not to be doubted. This should not, however, obscure the fact that the parallels are equally and often more striking in Assyrian and Egyptian religion.

[3] הֲרִאישׁוֹן אָדָם תִּוָּלֵד וְלִפְנֵי גְבָעוֹת חוֹלָלְתָּ

Are you the first Man that was born?
Or were you brought forth before the hills?

The words רִאשׁוֹן אָדָם...lead the thought...to the myth of the Primeval Man. That this myth has been known in Israel, is proved by the song about the King of Tyre in Ezek. xxviii. 1–19 (especially *vv.* 12 ff.).[1] For this song alludes unmistakably to the idea of the first man, living in glory like a god in Paradise, which is here thought to be situated on the mount of the gods. This Primeval Man is endowed with extraordinary wisdom (*vv.* 12, 17...). Later Jewish tradition refers this passage to Adam, who is expressly described as being very wise. Moreover, the great wisdom of Primeval Man is a very common motive [*sic*], found already in the Babylonian myth of Adapa but also e.g. in the Son of man in the Book of Enoch.[2]

Thus, whereas previously *Word* and *Wisdom* have been found so closely associated as often to be indistinguishable, now Wisdom is found related to *Anthropos* at an early date.

It is equally interesting when Ringgren finds Wisdom as a 'hypostasis in the making' in connection with a *berachah*, the Jewish antecedent to the Christian thanksgiving that apparently provides the context for the New Testament Christological hymns. bBerakot 58 b:[3]

ברוך אשר חלק מחכמתו ליראיו

Blessed is He who distributed of His wisdom to them that fear Him.[4]

Wisdom is then further hypostatized when, in Sir. xxiv, she 'is said to have come forth from the mouth of God and is thus

[1] 'Son of man, raise a lamentation over the King of Tyre, and say to him, Thus says the Lord God:
"You were the signet of perfection [?]
full of wisdom
and perfect in beauty.
You were in Eden, the garden of God;
every precious stone was your covering,

. . . .

On the day that you were created
they were prepared."'
[2] Ringgren, pp. 90 f. Cf. further W. D. Davies, *Paul and Rabbinic Judaism. Some Rabbinic Elements in Pauline Theology*, rev. edn (New York and Evanston, 1967), p. 45; and Robin Scroggs, *The Last Adam. A Study in Pauline Anthropology* (Philadelphia, 1966), p. 10 n. 26.   [3] Cited by Ringgren, p. 107.
[4] Thus Dürr's association of the Word with what he loosely named *berachoth* is here in a fashion confirmed for the term *berachah* properly used, since Wisdom, in an early stage of hypostatization, is associated with a *berachah* and is then, in a somewhat more advanced stage, not clearly distinguished from the Word.

identified with the word (v. 3a)'.[1] Ringgren summarizes his views about the origin of Sophia:

the process of hypostatization is in my opinion the very origin of the figure of Wisdom. But by this I have not intended to deny that foreign influence has asserted itself in the formation of Wisdom as a personal being. As a matter of fact, most of the concrete features in Wisdom can be shown to reflect mythological ideas.[2]

The general picture with regard to Wisdom

In order to try to show the relation between natural hypostatization and influence from other religions, Ringgren next discusses the various parallels to the Jewish Sophia in the context of the larger environment of the religions of the ancient world. Thus there is the Mesopotamian goddess Šiduri-Sabitu, who is called 'Ishtar of wisdom and the guardian spirit of life'.[3] There is also the possibility that Ḥukm (=wisdom) is a name of 'the old Semitic solar mother-deity';[4] and the Odes of Solomon, which Ringgren sees as having a strong relationship to the Old Testament and to Jewish Wisdom literature in particular, seem to him to be influenced by Babylonian concepts concerning wisdom. 'Ea, the lord of the waters and the sea, was also the lord of wisdom...In the Odes of Solomon the water of life is at the same time the water of wisdom.'[5] There are also, on the other hand, strong parallels between the Jewish Sophia and Isis. Thus 'Reitzenstein...maintained a definite relation between late Egyptian Isis speculation and the Jewish doctrine of Wisdom',[6] and although

it is not necessary to assume an Egyptian prototype of the figure of Wisdom in Job and Proverbs...it is probable that the self-praise of Isis has been known to the author of Sirach, and he has intended to make the self-praise of Wisdom in ch. xxiv an Israelitic counterpart to the Egyptian, and to show that Israelitic Wisdom possessed the merits for which Isis was praised.[7]

---

[1] Ringgren, p. 108. [2] *Ibid.* pp. 132 f.
[3] *Ištar nīmēki šēdu balāṭi* (*ibid.* p. 137). [4] *Ibid.* p. 138 n. 1.
[5] *Ibid.* p. 141.
[6] Reitzenstein, *Zwei religionsgeschichtliche Fragen*, pp. 104 f.
[7] Ringgren, p. 146. This relationship was earlier noted by W. L. Knox, *St Paul and the Church of the Gentiles* (Cambridge, 1939), pp. 55 f., and 'The Divine Wisdom', *JTS*, vol. xxxviii (1937), pp. 230 f. So now, in extensive

Ringgren, however, cautiously avoids voicing a decisive opinion concerning influence of foreign religions on the hypostatization of Wisdom in Judaism. 'To sum up, we might say that the general idea of a goddess has influenced the shaping of personal Wisdom, whether it be from a Hellenistic Isis religion, from an Astarte influenced by Isis, or from a general Semitic Ishtar-Astarte.'[1] Other Old Testament and Jewish hypostases, which may be explained similarly, are אמת, truth, and חסד, steadfast love.[2]

Hypostatization of the Word

Ringgren considers the Old Testament Word to be 'a concretion of the divine word as a breath from the mouth of God or a substance full of power'; and he follows Dürr in seeing a true hypostasis of the Word in the Old Testament, for 'we find... the divine word, emanating from the divinity, as bearer of the divine power, obviously separate from God and yet belonging to him, a hypostasis in the proper sense of the word'.[3]

Ringgren improves on Dürr's study by following this hypostatization of the Word into the area of the Targums and of rabbinic literature, where the Word is respectively the מֵימְרָא or the דִּבּוּר (or דיברא). Thus in the Targums one reads, 'Yahweh's *mēmrā* sits upon His throne high and lifted up, and hears our prayer'; 'Hear, o *mēmrā* of Yahweh, the voice of Judah's prayer'; and again 'I by my *mēmrā* have made the earth'.[4] This last is particularly interesting, since it so nearly parallels John i. 10: ὁ κόσμος δι' αὐτοῦ [*sc.* τοῦ λόγου] ἐγένετο, where the Aramaic בְּ is equivalent to the Greek διά. In the rabbinic literature

---

agreement with Reitzenstein, Knox, and Ringgren, Hans Conzelmann, 'Die Mutter der Weisheit', *Zeit und Geschichte. Dankesgabe an Rudolf Bultmann zum 80. Geburtstag*, ed. Erich Dinkler (Tübingen, 1964), pp. 225–34.

[1] Ringgren, p. 147. A good brief summary of the role of Wisdom in Judaism is given by Davies, pp. 163–9.

[2] Ringgren, pp. 150, 171.   [3] *Ibid.* p. 159.

[4] Deut. iv. 7, JerT I; Deut. xxxiii. 7, JerT II; Isa. xlv. 12; cited by Ringgren, p. 162. In view of such statements, it is difficult to understand George Foot Moore's statement (*Judaism in the First Centuries of the Christian Era. The Age of the Tannaim*, vol. I (Cambridge, 1944), pp. 417 f.) that 'where the "word of God" in the Hebrew Scriptures is the medium or instrumentality of revelation or of communication with men, it is not in the Targums his *memra*; nor is the creative word of God his *memra*'.

Shekinah replaces Memra, thus obscuring the association with the Logos of John i, but 'we have a direct equivalent to Memra in דִּבּוּר (or דיברא)'. This, too, appears personified. Shir Hashirim r. 1, 2, 2:

> The Word emerged from the right hand of the Holy One, blessed be He, and went to the right of Israel; thence returning it surrounded the camp of Israel...Thence returning it went from the right of Israel to the right of [God], and [God] received it on His right, and engraved it on the tablet; and its voice resounded from one end of the world to the other.

The *dibbūr* is also hypostatized in the Talmud, where it is said, regarding Ps. xxxiii. 6: 'From each word that proceeded from the mouth of the Holy One, blessed be He, there was created an angel, for it is said: "By the word of the Lord were the Heavens made; and all their host by the breath of his mouth."'[1]

In some respects, the solution given by Dürr and Ringgren to the problem of the historical religious background of the prologue of John is more satisfactory than that of Bultmann. Here one does not have to suppose a highly developed myth that was 'reduced', and the texts seem to show clearly that the progressive hypostatization of the Word in Judaism, constantly under influence from foreign religions, comes close enough to what is said of the Logos in the prologue of John that the prologue may be seen as merely the next stage in this process. One might object that Bultmann's conjecture of a pre-Christian gnostic redeemer myth gives a more satisfactory explanation to the dualistic elements in the prologue of John; but one would have to recall that Iranian dualism had made an impact on at least one other group within Judaism around the beginning of the Christian era, as passages in the Dead Sea Scrolls attest[2]— here precisely without the myth of a redeemer. The addition of this dualism to the hypostatized, Sophia-like Logos could account for everything said of the Logos in the prologue of John except the incarnation, which would then be the Christian addition made in appropriating the myth as an explanation of

---

[1] bHagiga 14a; quoted by Ringgren, p. 164.

[2] The best known such passage is of course 1QS iii–iv. Cf. e.g. the diagrammatic making explicit of the dualism in this passage by Davies, 'Paul and the Dead Sea Scrolls: Flesh and Spirit', *The Scrolls and the New Testament*, ed. Krister Stendahl (New York, 1957), pp. 171 f.

the salvation event in Christ. But then there would have been a pre-Christian gnostic redeemer myth! Or did Christianity provide both the dualism and the incarnation? In spite of the fact that the Fourth Gospel also employs this dualism, the seeming quoted character of at least *vv.* 1–5 and 9–11 would tend to give weight to the assumption that Christianity, or at least the author of the Fourth Gospel, provided only the concept of incarnation.

If only the prologue of John were involved, one would perhaps be content to let the matter rest here; but there is the problem that the other New Testament Christological hymns, which do not mention the Logos,[1] are so closely related to the prologue of John. This necessitates some kind of unified explanation of the historical religious background of all the hymns together, not of any one in isolation.

[1] With the possible exception that Heb. i. 3, with its mention of the ῥῆμα, shows an indirect relation to the Logos motif.

CHAPTER 3

PHILIPPIANS ii. 6–11

THE SUFFERING SERVANT

Lohmeyer's interest in this hymn was primarily with its 'religious meaning', but in order to analyze the passage from that point of view he found it necessary to discuss to some extent the religious parallels. These parallels he found for the most part in Judaism, particularly in the Servant Song of Isa. lii. 13–liii. 12.[1] The apocalyptic Son of man, however, was seen to stand even more prominently in the background, and Lohmeyer cited as chief evidence of this the phrase ὡς ἄνθρωπος in Phil. ii. 8, which he explained as being an exact translation of the Aramaic כבר־אנש.[2] This explanation of ὡς ἄνθρωπος has, however, never been accepted, and falls on the ground that no examples can be cited for such a translation.[3] Lohmeyer also saw other concepts from Hellenistic Judaism, particularly Logos and Kyrios, as having been incorporated into the hymn by its author, and he concluded that 'the concepts of this psalm stand in the middle

[1] Lohmeyer, *Kyrios Jesus*, pp. 33, 36. A fairly exhaustive history of the interpretation of Phil. ii. 6–11 is given by R. P. Martin, *Carmen Christi. Philippians ii. 5–11 in Recent Interpretation and in the Setting of Early Christian Worship* (SNTS Monograph Series, 4) (Cambridge, 1967), pp. 63–95.

[2] Lohmeyer, *Kyrios Jesus*, pp. 39 f.

[3] Lohmeyer cited Rev. i. 13 and xiv. 14; but here the Greek reads ὅμοιος υἱὸς ἀνθρώπου (some MSS read υἱῷ). Both ὡς ἄνθρωπος, of course, and ὅμοιος υἱὸς ἀνθρώπου would be 'exact' translations of כבר־אנש, and both are Semitizing translations—the one in the use of ὡς, the other in the retention of the 'son'. Yet it is the absence of the word 'son' from Phil. ii. 8 that prevents concluding with certainty that ὡς ἄνθρωπος translates the required Aramaic idiom—all the more so in view of the normal retention of the word 'son' in the New Testament. We probably see here only one more example of the influence of Semitic languages on the Greek of the New Testament. Since Lohmeyer's suggestion about the Son of man did not prove correct, it does not matter whether there *was* such a figure in apocalyptic Judaism or not. Cf. Norman Perrin, *Rediscovering the Teaching of Jesus* (New York and Evanston, 1967), pp. 164–73. Cf. further Geza Vermes, 'The Use of בר נש/בר נשא in Jewish Aramaic', *An Aramaic Approach to the Gospels and Acts*, by Matthew Black (Oxford, 1967³), pp. 327 f.

between the Jewish Son of man doctrine and the Johannine Logos speculation'.[1]

Later investigations into the historical religious background of the prologue of John would, as ch. 2 shows, tend to corroborate this view of Lohmeyer's, if only as a starting point for further investigation. Such a possibility was sidetracked, however, by the raising of the influence of the concept of the Suffering Servant to a position of supreme importance for the understanding of Phil. ii. 6–11. This was first done by Lucien Cerfaux,[2] who defined his position in this way:

> The contrast between the humiliation and the exaltation of Christ, which furnishes the subject of the hymn, is inspired by the song of the servant of God (Isa. lii. 13–liii. 12)...Each one of the strophes presents literary contacts with this passage, and the two parallel lines of the third strophe ('that every knee may bow' and 'every tongue confess') are borrowed textually from Isa. xlv. 23.[3]

It is a problem that the Servant of God is usually designated παῖς in Greek, whereas Phil. ii. 7 employs the word δοῦλος, but Cerfaux observed that 'Aquila (Isa. lii. 13) translates δοῦλος, and the Septuagint itself writes δουλεύοντα in the context (lii. 11)'. His explanation for the use of δοῦλος instead of παῖς in the Philippians hymn was that it made more pointed the antithesis to κύριος. He further thought that Deutero-Isaiah had provided the idea for the clause ἑαυτὸν ἐκένωσεν, unique in Paul, since Isa. xlix. 4 LXX reads κενῶς ἐκοπίασα καὶ εἰς μάταιον καὶ εἰς οὐδὲν ἔδωκα τὴν ἰσχύν μου; and 'the essential word, ἐταπείνωσεν, echoes ἐν τῇ ταπεινώσει of Isaiah (liii. 8)'.[4]

With ὡς ἄνθρωπος Cerfaux compared Isa. liii. 3: τὸ εἶδος αὐτοῦ ἄτιμον ἐκλεῖπον παρὰ πάντας ἀνθρώπους, ἄνθρωπος ἐν πληγῇ ὤν; and μέχρι θανάτου 'answers in the Servant song [to] ἤχθη εἰς θάνατον (liii. 8) and παρεδόθη εἰς θάνατον (liii. 12)'.[5] Cerfaux summarized:

> It seems that we are able to comprehend the manner of working of the author of the Christological hymn. The song of the Servant furnished the theme. The Christ has taken the role of the Servant, he

[1] Lohmeyer, *Kyrios Jesus*, p. 77.
[2] Lucien Cerfaux, 'L'hymne au Christ-Serviteur de Dieu (*Phil.*, II, 6–11 = *Is.*, LII, 13–LIII, 12)', *Miscellanea historica in honorem Alberti de Meyer* (Louvain, 1946), vol. I, pp. 117–30.
[3] *Ibid.* p. 118. [4] *Ibid.* pp. 120 f. [5] *Ibid.* pp. 121 f.

is the Servant of God of whom Isaiah was the preacher. Doubtless the idea that the Servant is a divine being should have been explicated. But does not the Servant, in Isaiah itself, loom up brusquely, like a divine being (cf. xlix. 1–2)?[1]

Not only did Cerfaux think that the ideas of Phil. ii. 6–11 came entirely from Isaiah, but he even found formal similarities between the Philippians hymn and the Servant passages in Deutero-Isaiah. 'The opening of the third strophe, "wherefore", corresponds to the turning point in the Servant Song, liii. 12, "Wherefore he shall receive many things as an inheritance;"'[2] and even the Name of Phil. ii. 9 is to be related to the Servant. 'One has noted ἕνεκεν κυρίου (xlix. 7) and καλέσω σε τῷ ὀνόματί μου (xlv. 4).'[3]

It is possible, however, to relate this hymn even more closely to the Isaianic passage. Joachim Jeremias, in the section of *The Servant of God*[4] entitled 'Christological Interpretations of the Deutero-Isaiah Servant of God in the New Testament', says, 'The connexion of Phil. ii. 6–11 with Isa. liii becomes plain as soon as it is recognized that not the LXX but the Heb. text of Isa. liii is used.'[5] Thus the word δοῦλος, rather than the Septuagintal παῖς, renders עֶבֶד of Isa. lii. 13. And 'the decisive proof of the connexion of Phil ii. 6–11 with Isa. liii lies in the fact that the expression ἑαυτὸν ἐκένωσεν (Phil. ii. 7), attested nowhere else in the Greek and grammatically extremely harsh, is an exact rendering of נַפְשׁוֹ...הֶעֱרָה (Isa. liii. 12)'.[6]

---

[1] *Ibid.* p. 122.   [2] *Ibid.*   [3] *Ibid.* p. 124.

[4] Walter Zimmerli and Joachim Jeremias, *The Servant of God*, trans. Harold Knight *et al.* (SBT, 20) (Naperville, Ill., 1957; being a translation of his article 'παῖς θεοῦ' in *TWNT*).

[5] *Ibid.* p. 97 n. 446: 'With μορφή (Phil. ii. 6, 7) is perhaps to be compared the rendering of תֹּאַר (Isa. lii. 14) with μορφή by 'A; with ἐταπείνωσεν ἑαυτόν (Phil. ii. 8), cf. the rendering of מְעֻנֶּה (Isa. liii. 4) by ταπεινοῦν in 'A, Σ, and Θ; regarding ὑπήκοος (Phil. ii. 8) cf. the rendering of נַעֲנֶה (Isa. liii. 7) with ὑπήκουσεν by Σ; with διό (Phil. ii. 9) cf. לָכֵן (Isa. liii. 12); with ὑπερύψωσεν (Phil. ii. 9) cf. יָרוּם וְנִשָּׂא וְגָבַהּ מְאֹד (Isa. liii. 13).' This explanation has been rather widely disputed; cf. now Deichgräber, p. 124, who does not find the Isaianic לָמוּת in the expression ἑαυτὸν ἐκένωσεν.

[6] Jeremias, *The Servant of God*, p. 97. Jeremias has again defended the view that ἑαυτὸν ἐκένωσεν is a direct translation of the Hebrew of Isa. liii. 12 in 'Zu Phil. ii 7: EAYTON EKENΩΣEN', *Novum Testamentum*, vol. VI (1963), pp. 182–8.

David Stanley has also maintained the Isaianic origin of this passage.[1] Not only does the hymn, as he understands the situation, 'derive its inspiration' from Isa. lii. 13–liii. 12, but also its 'terminology'.[2] Whereas Cerfaux had maintained Pauline authorship for the hymn, Stanley takes the opposite view, based on his observation that the usage of terms in the hymn is foreign to Paul's vocabulary.[3] He conjectures that it 'originated in the theological milieu of Pauline Christianity'.

This attempt to derive the concepts contained in the hymn in Phil. ii solely from the Old Testament seems to have a particular theological bias: that New Testament concepts which are not completely new with the New Testament must have been derived from the Old Testament; otherwise they cannot be acceptable to Christianity. The impropriety of this view must be discussed at another time and place. Here it is sufficient to point out that such an explanation of the relation of Christianity to the Old Testament ignores the fact that Old Testament concepts had themselves undergone considerable modification in Judaism both during and prior to the Roman period, and it thus obscures the immediate religious background of Phil. ii. 6–11.[4]

Rather than directly from the Old Testament itself, Eduard Schweizer does see this hymn as the product of a concept which had developed in Judaism and which was taken over into Christianity as the pattern of Christian existence. This concept is the pattern of humiliation and exaltation, which is found in Judaism primarily in connection with the Deutero-Isaianic Servant of God.[5] Schweizer summarizes this view:

[1] Stanley, 'The Theme of the Servant of Yahweh'.

[2] *Ibid.* pp. 421 f. Stanley merely briefly summarizes the views of Cerfaux.

[3] *Ibid.*; above, p. 10 n. 1.

[4] The alteration of the concept of the Servant between the time of Isa. liii and the time of the New Testament is clearly seen by Ziener, p. 120, who points out that the presentation of Jesus as the Righteous One in Matt. xxvii. 19; Acts iii. 14; vii. 52; and xxii. 14 is to be understood in terms of the Righteous One of Sapientia, and not 'merely' in terms of Isa. liii. Further typical of those who understand the concepts of Isa. liii to have been brought directly over and applied to Jesus (by himself!) are Dodd, *The Bible Today* (Cambridge, 1946), pp. 94 f., and Davies, *Paul and Rabbinic Judaism*, pp. 274 f.

[5] Schweizer, *Erniedrigung und Erhöhung*.

The picture of the suffering and exalted Righteous One...determined the congregation's view of Christ prior to and contemporary with Paul. It is at the same time to be affirmed that neither Jesus himself nor his disciples ever viewed their master merely as *one* of the many suffering Righteous Ones. Certainly, none of these suffering Righteous Ones called disciples to follow him. None expected that it will befall Sodom and Gomorrha better than those who do not hear his call. None explained that the disciple following him must give up father and mother, wife and child, hand and foot, even his own life, in order just in that way to find life. Jesus was always *the* Righteous One for them.[1]

Throughout the New Testament, as Schweizer interprets it, Jesus is understood in terms of the self-abasement of the Servant of God, and this concept was finally, in Phil. ii. 6–8, expanded to apply to his pre-existence.[2] Regarding Phil. ii. 6–11, Schweizer points out that already in apocalyptic Judaism the concept of the Servant was attached to an idea of exaltation and enthronement:

According to the Similitudes of Ethiopic Enoch, the 'Elect One' abides with the Lord of Spirits as head of the elect Righteous Ones (xxxix. 6 f.; cf. xl. 5)...On 'that day'...he will sit 'on the throne of glory', even as 'the Exalted One' on 'God's throne', and will hold court (xlv. 3; xlix. 4; lxi. 8; lxix. 27)...All inhabitants of the earth, even kings and powers, will then recognize the long hidden Son of man on the throne of his glory, and will be astonished at him, and will worship him (xlviii. 5; lxii. 1–7).

Thus Schweizer seems to propose that the Deutero-Isaianic Servant and the apocalyptic Son of man were identified in pre-Christian Judaism.[3]

[1] *Ibid.* pp. 61 f.

[2] *Ibid.* p. 99. The view e.g. of Davies, *Paul and Rabbinic Judaism*, pp. 265 f., that the obedience mentioned in our passage is to the Torah is of course possible, but one must only note that the passage contains no reference to the Torah. Davies' implied point (*ibid.* pp. 227–84) that the reference to death as obedience involves a sacrificial understanding of obedient death may be true for the Pauline gloss in *v.* 8, but not for the original hymn; cf. Lohmeyer, *Kyrios Jesus*, pp. 44 f.

[3] Schweizer, *Erniedrigung und Erhöhung*, p. 30. However closely the Son of man is associated with righteousness in I Enoch, he is not identified with the Servant. What takes place is rather that one figure begins to assume the functions of another. (Thus, the statement of Davies, *Paul and Rabbinic Judaism*, pp. 279 f., that 'it is clear that the Son of Man in the Similitudes is

Schweizer defines μορφὴ δούλου according to the classical meaning, 'kind', by which the interpretation of μορφή as essence is excluded, and asks if this is not closer to Old Testament thought, which 'did not at all distinguish form and matter like the Greeks, but bound the essence of a thing together with its appearance'.[1] He cites Gen. i. 26, in which man, as Lord of the world, is the εἰκών (synonymous with μορφή) of God, and says that 'things, according to the late Jewish view, lost this condition of similarity to God through the fall. Only through the Messiah will it be reestablished eschatologically.' Finally, Schweizer sees the exaltation in Phil. ii. 9 as stemming from Ps. xcvii. 9: σὺ εἶ κύριος ὁ ὕψιστος...ὑπερυψώθης.[2] Schweizer recognizes the close relation between Phil. ii. 6–8 and Jewish Wisdom, but concludes that the present hymn goes beyond the 'concept of Wisdom' and is closer to the suffering Righteous One.[3]

Schweizer has thus brought to attention several elements

merged to some extent at least into the concept of the Suffering Messiah' is still too strong. So also with regard to the view of William Manson, *Jesus the Messiah. The Synoptic Tradition of the Revelation of God in Christ: With Special Reference to Form-Criticism* (London, 1943), p. 174, that such texts give evidence of '*successive phases of the Messianic idea*'. Here, 'Messianic idea' is far too loosely defined.) Sapientia is in this respect very close to Enoch. Thus Ziener, p. 113, points out that here 'Wisdom embraces all divine gifts and powers that operate among men', whereas earlier God's Spirit had fulfilled this function (cf. Isa. lxiii. 11 ff.; Zech. vii. 12). Also, to Sophia is 'ascribed what is otherwise said of the Messiah' (*ibid.* p. 115; with Isa. xi. 1 ff., cf. Prov. viii. 12 ff.; with Ps. ii. 8; lxxii. 8, cf. Sap. viii. 1; with Ps. cx. 1, cf. Sap. ix. 4). Thus Ps. ii. 8 seems to put all of creation in the possession of the Messiah, whereas Prov. viii. 22 makes Sophia the ἀρχή of God's way. Also, with the Son of man in Daniel should be compared Sap. vii. 29 f.; viii. 1; cf. A. Feuillet, 'Le Fils de l'homme de Daniel et la tradition biblique', *RB*, vol. LX (1953), pp. 323 and 334. Schweizer states (*Erniedrigung und Erhöhung*, p. 31), 'In IV Ezra the Messiah is the Servant of God (vii. 28; xiii. 32; xiv. 9).' This statement apparently rests on the fact that the Messiah is called 'my Son' in these three passages, and on the assumption that 'Son' renders παῖς = עבד. Such an assumption is highly problematical, however, given (*a*) the absence of Greek MSS for IV Ezra, (*b*) the composite nature of the work, and (*c*) the several textual variants for vii. 28. The assumption of Deichgräber, p. 131, that the 'motif of humiliation and suffering stemming from Isa. liii' indicates the concept of a dying Son of man is, in view of the several discussions reported on here, naive.

[1] Schweizer, *Erniedrigung und Erhöhung*, p. 98 n. 389.
[2] *Ibid.* [3] *Ibid.* pp. 100 f.

from Judaism that seem in some way to be related to the unified concept that is presented in the hymn of Phil. ii. 6–11. How such elements came together in a hymnic tradition that led not only to the Philippians hymn but also to the other New Testament Christological hymns is, however, not adequately answered.[1]

THE TWO ADAMS: JEAN HÉRING

Quite another possibility for explaining the historical religious background of Phil. ii. 6–11 was suggested in 1936 by Jean Héring,[2] who saw the passage as an expression of the 'anthropo-sophia' of Philonic Judaism. Héring called attention to Rom. v. 12–21 and I Cor. xv. 45–9, in which 'the apostle expresses the soteriological role of Jesus within the framework of the specula-tion about the Anthropos or Adam. Yet the notion of the Anthropos indicates here a polarity, unknown to Daniel, Enoch, and Jesus, but presupposed... by Philo.'[3]

[1] Feuillet has sought to show ('L'hymne christologique de l'épître aux Philippiens (II, 6–11)', *RB*, vol. LXXII (1965), pp. 325–80, 481–507) that the hymn can be understood solely from the Old Testament (and its Jewish interpretation). He finds the influence of Isa. lii. 13–liii. 12 the strongest, and in general accepts the views of Jeremias (*ibid.* pp. 357–9). Joined with this influence, however, is that of Adam, which is seen to be both a positive and negative influence; positive in that the Christ of Phil. ii. 6, like the Adam of Gen. iii. 5, is not to grasp equality with God, negative in that Christ's obedience, as in Rom. v. 19, is contrasted to Adam's disobedience (*ibid.* pp. 367 f.). Taking the Son of man to be equated with the Messiah in the Similitudes of Enoch, Feuillet further (*ibid.* pp. 377 f.) thinks that there is a possibility that the Son of man of apocalypticism may have influenced the conceptuality of the hymn. But where did such varied motifs run together? What of intervening Jewish cosmological and mythological speculation, not to mention the process of hypostatization? Feuillet's state-ment that Wisdom is 'totally foreign to Phil. ii. 6–11' (*ibid.* p. 380) seems to draw the conclusions too simply and too hastily. In support of the view that reference to Isa. lii. 13–liii. 12 fails to explain the conceptuality of the present hymn, cf. further Morna D. Hooker, *Jesus and the Servant. The Influence of the Servant Concept of Deutero-Isaiah in the New Testament* (London, 1959), pp. 120 f.

[2] Jean Héring, 'Kyrios Anthropos', *RHPR*, vol. VI (1936), pp. 196–209. Cf. further the review in Martin, *Carmen Christi*, pp. 161–4.

[3] *Ibid.* p. 197; cf. *Leg. Alleg.* i. 31 (Gen. ii. 7 is cited): ὁ μὲν γάρ ἐστιν οὐράνιος ἄνθρωπος, ὁ δὲ γήινος. ὁ μὲν οὖν οὐράνιος ἅτε κατ' εἰκόνα θεοῦ γεγονὼς φθαρτῆς καὶ συνόλως γεώδους οὐσίας ἀμέτοχος, ὁ δὲ γήινος ἐκ σποράδος ὕλης, ἣν χοῦν κέκληκεν, ἐπάγη· διὸ τὸν μὲν οὐράνιόν φησιν οὐ

The concepts of the earthly and the heavenly man, then—which were already beginning to blend together in Philo and in Paul—were seen by Héring as united in the figure of the redeemer in Phil. ii. 6–11. 'It goes without saying that it is a question here of the heavenly man, and the fact is that Philo has equally accorded to that man the narrative of the creation of Gen. i.'[1] Thus, going farther than Philo, who merely brought the two together in the same discussion, the hymn of Phil. ii *combines*, in Héring's opinion, the concept of the heavenly Adam of Gen. i, who was in the form of God and was associated with creation, with that of the earthly Adam of Gen. iii, who succumbs to the temptation to be like God, and thus must humble himself. 'The one of the two men, by his pride, brought about his own downfall as well as that of the universe; the other reconciled the world to God and was elevated by him.'[2]

Héring thought that it was the concept of the Lord which had brought these two Adams together. ''Ἄνθρωπος and Κύριος; here then are the two foci of the Christological ellipse. The pre-existence and the incarnation of the Savior are represented within the framework of Adamic speculation, while the notion of Kyrios permits taking account of the eminent position of Christ in the cult as well as his cosmic role.'[3]

This interpretation, that *vv.* 6–8 refer to the two Adams, the heavenly and the earthly, allowed Héring to interpret *v.* 7 as speaking still of the pre-existent one, yet referring to his (earthly) submission:

It is precisely because Jesus was already Man in his pre-existence that he was prepared for the incarnation and for his role as firstborn of the dead, and, thereby, as leader of a new humanity...In spite of the Kenosis an essential element of his essence subsists, his character as *Anthropos*. The change which is accomplished in him consists in the transformation of a heavenly man into an earthly man.[4]

πεπλάσθαι, κατ' εἰκόνα δὲ τετυπῶσθαι θεοῦ, τὸν δὲ γήινον πλάσμα, ἀλλ' οὐ γέννημα, εἶναι τοῦ τεχνίτου; and *de Opificio Mundi* 134:...τοῦ...πλασθέντος ἀνθρώπου καὶ τοῦ κατὰ τὴν εἰκόνα θεοῦ γεγονότος πρότερον· ὁ μὲν γὰρ διαπλασθεὶς αἰσθητὸς ἤδη μετέχων ποιότητος, ἐκ σώματος καὶ ψυχῆς συνεστώς, ἀνὴρ ἢ γυνή, φύσει θνητός· ὁ δὲ κατὰ τὴν εἰκόνα ἰδέα τις ἢ γένος ἢ σφραγίς, νοητός, ἀσώματος, οὔτ' ἄρρεν οὔτε θῆλυ, ἄφθαρτος φύσει.

[1] Héring, p. 201. [2] *Ibid.* pp. 202 f.
[3] *Ibid.* p. 204. [4] *Ibid.* p. 205.

Héring's solution has in its favor the fact that it suits the strophic arrangement later proposed by Jeremias. It also allows a smooth transition to be made between stanzas one and two. Such a solution also has its problems, however, since the presence of ἐν ὁμοιώματι ἀνθρώπων γενόμενος in *v.* 7 (the beginning of Jeremias' second stanza) would seem to indicate that this would have to be the *first* appearance of Adam/ Anthropos in the hymn; or, in other words, that the redeemer here first becomes Man. Also, of course, the concept of the man who by his pride brought sin into the world is not present in the hymn, but only felt to be there.[1] Héring's explanation has pointed out, however, that in Hellenistic Judaism, at least for Philo, the Old Testament concept of the first man could be so explained that the heavenly Anthropos begins to acquire the character of an independent, eternal divine being, i.e. to resemble the Logos or the Sophia.

THE GNOSTIC REDEEMER: ERNST KÄSEMANN

One of the most thorough recent studies of Phil. ii. 6–11 is that of Ernst Käsemann.[2] In his lengthy essay, Käsemann not only gives a complete review of modern German scholarship dealing with this hymn, but discusses the interpretation of each section, including comments dealing with the religious milieu from which the ideas in the hymn came. It is only his understanding of the religious background of the concepts contained in this hymn that will be discussed here.

Käsemann begins by characterizing the Hellenistic period:

The terminology of the Hellenistic period stands in a system which, with regard to the view of the world from which it coordinates things, is different from the system of classical Greece. This can also

---

[1] Héring, to be sure, is not the only one to suggest that Phil. ii. 6–11 refers to Christ as the second Adam. One may mention further C. K. Barrett, *From First Adam to Last. A Study in Pauline Theology* (New York, 1962), pp. 16, 69–72, and Davies, *Paul and Rabbinic Judaism*, pp. 41 f. (cf. also the other authors referred to there). The caution of one of Davies' pupils, however, is worthy of note: of non-Pauline New Testament texts, 'only Col. i. 15–20; Phil. ii. 5–11; and Mark i. 9–11 could be considered Adamic in background, and not even these are certain' (Scroggs, p. 115 n. 2; cf. further pp. 89 f., 99).

[2] Käsemann, 'Kritische Analyse von Phil. 2, 5–11'.

be clearly seen precisely in the anthropological terminology, that between the two epochs there lies a structural change in the world-view.

When the polis ceased to exist, the view of the cosmos changed, in that the chaos was seen as breaking into the realm of order. This meant that there was constant war with the powers, and 'the earth [was] no longer the object which [was] bounded and formed by the Logos'.[1] It was to this situation that the mysteries spoke. 'The world no longer [held] its salvation in its own hand. It [stood] under Ananke, and only he who [brought] it release from Ananke [might] grant it salvation.' In this environment, the terms 'form' and 'matter' no longer meant what they had in classical Greece. Consequently, any term related to them, e.g. μορφή, would also have an altered meaning.[2] In this world ruled by ἀνάγκη, μορφή has come to designate essence. 'But essence is now seen in a different perspective,' and the phrase ἐν μορφῇ 'indicates the realm in which one stands and which determines one like a force field. It is in this way that Hellenism views existence; at any given time it is placed in a force field and thereby qualified.'[3]

Such a concept, expressed also by the phrase ἴσα θεῷ and by the θεὸς ἦν of John i. 1, cannot have come into the Philippians hymn from Judaism, for 'all of Judaism [answers], No one is

[1] *Ibid.* pp. 65 f.

[2] *Ibid.* p. 66. Johannes Behm, in his article 'μορφή, etc.', *TDNT*, vol. IV, ed. Gerhard Kittel, trans. and ed. Geoffrey W. Bromiley (Grand Rapids, Michigan, 1967), pp. 743 f., claimed that this term 'in its fundamental meaning is synon. with εἶδος, ἰδέα and σχῆμα'. Yet, 'μορφή differs from σχῆμα inasmuch as it indicates the individual appearance as it is, while σχῆμα refers to its outward representation. μορφή is the whole (of the body etc.) in and for itself, while σχῆμα is what belongs or has ref. to the whole.' Thus the term μορφὴ δούλου in Phil. ii. 7 is seen to indicate 'an act of exemplary restraint on the part of Christ,...a concrete demonstration of this restraint' (*ibid.* p. 750). A transformation, a metamorphosis is not therefore indicated; rather 'as the One who became man...He bore the figure or form of a slave, of a being which is wholly dependent on the will of another' (*ibid.*). μορφὴ θεοῦ does not, in Behm's opinion, mean οὐσία or φύσις; and he sees Phil. ii. 6–11 as the creation of the apostle, not as originating in a myth (*ibid.* p. 752). It is against this explanation of the classical definition of μορφή that Käsemann directs his explanation of the definition of μορφή in the Hellenistic period.

[3] Käsemann, 'Kritische Analyse von Phil. 2, 5–11', p. 68.

like unto thee'. Käsemann thus finds a parallel for this exclusive usage in Hellenistic religion; *Corp. Herm.* i. 13 f.: ἔδειξε...τὴν καλὴν τοῦ θεοῦ μορφήν. 'That would nevertheless mean that the tradition of the myth of the divine primal Man, which certainly plays a most meaningful role in the New Testament, has influenced at least the terminology of our text as well.' The term εἰκών of God in Col. i. 15 Käsemann also considers to mean materially the same as μορφή of God here, and the occurrence of this concept in several different places points back, in his opinion, to 'the same context of the doctrine of the primal Man-Redeemer, which was taken over from Gnosticism and made useful for New Testament Christology'.[1]

In the cosmic drama which is the subject of the hymn, *v.* 7 *a* speaks already of the redeemer's becoming man; ἐκένωσεν means 'God became man...no more and no less',[2] for μορφὴ δούλου is the opposite of μορφὴ θεοῦ. As he was once the same as God, now the redeemer is the same as man; but this means that he is the slave of εἱμαρμένη, 'of matter, of stars and powers'.[3] Käsemann thus understands the gnostic redeemer here in terms of the second Adam. 'Just as Adam's disobedience had brought death and curse to the whole world, the obedience of Christ brought life and justice into the world and thereby *restitutio in integrum.*'[4]

That ὑπερύψωσεν places the obedient one in the highest position seems to Käsemann to show that this refers to exaltation and not to resurrection, and 'this nuance has the material sense of presenting Christ as cosmocrator'.[5] It is the confluence of Old Testament and Hellenistic terminology that makes him more than a mere cultic hero or lord; he is cosmocrator, lord of the cosmos, for the powers in *v.* 10 are cosmic powers.[6] Thus

[1] *Ibid.* pp. 69–71. [2] *Ibid.* pp. 71 f.

[3] Günther Bornkamm ('Zum Verständnis des Christus-Hymnus Phil. 2, 6–11') agrees with this interpretation of μορφὴ δούλου and rightly observes (*ibid.* p. 180), against Jeremias, that the death of the redeemer is first spoken of only at the end of *v.* 8. Bornkamm sees the hymn as Christian, and takes a cautious view toward all suggestions of an historical religious background, although he grants the presence of some gnostic elements in the hymn.

[4] Käsemann, 'Kritische Analyse von Phil. 2, 5–11', p. 80.

[5] This thesis of Käsemann's has found further—and more detailed—support in an essay by Siegfried Schulz, 'Maranatha und Kyrios Jesus', *ZNW*, vol. LIII (1962), pp. 125–44, particularly p. 128.

[6] Käsemann, 'Kritische Analyse von Phil. 2, 5–11', pp. 83–6.

does 'Christ take the place of Ananke...He is now the Panto-crator, whom all powers and authorities must serve and who unites in his all-comprehensive power what previously pressed apart and against one another in the opposition of powers and force fields. He is the "reconciler of the All", as in Col. i. 20.'[1] In this picture Käsemann sees yet one other element, 'the myth of the enthroned redeemer', which is attested in the fourth Eclogue of Virgil.[2]

Käsemann, then, thinks that this hymn is the creation of the early Church, in which such divergent motifs as those of the gnostic primal Man-Redeemer, the second Adam, the cultic lord of the Hellenistic world,[3] and consequently the Jewish concept of God as Lord have come together. Thus he has taken up again the line of investigation begun by Lohmeyer, and has seen a confluence in this hymn of several not unrelated mythical motifs from the Hellenistic world. The primary figure in this new configuration is the gnostic redeemer, but it is the com-munity's experience of Christ as Lord that brings the various themes into a unified whole. In this, Käsemann seems to have understood the hypothesis of a pre-Christian gnostic redeemer myth in a more general way than was the case with Bultmann, and this understanding consequently allows him to make better sense out of the interrelatedness between Phil. ii. 6–11 and the other Christological hymns. Yet, is it necessary, as Käsemann does, to explain this myth as Hellenistic *as distinct from Jewish*, particularly when it has been seen in the discussion of the prologue of John how nearly a hypostasis in Judaism approxi-mates the hypothetical pre-Christian gnostic redeemer? And does Käsemann not too readily exclude all influence from the Jewish concept of the Servant—to be sure, in an attempt to be more true to history than the proponents of influence from Isa. lii. 13–liii. 12, who see the matter of such influence in an unrealistically direct way? If one must object against the proponents of influence from the Deutero-Isaianic Servant that they have tended to overlook the further development of this concept in Judaism prior to Christianity, may this objection not be equally valid against Käsemann, albeit from the other side?

[1] *Ibid.* p. 88. [2] *Ibid.* Cf. Virgil, *Ecloga* iv. 15 f.
[3] *Ibid.* p. 84.

SERVANT AND WISDOM: DIETER GEORGI

In his essay in the third Bultmann *Festschrift*, Dieter Georgi has offered a third alternative for explaining the historical religious background of Phil. ii. 6–11, which is at the same time somewhat of a synthesis, as well as being to a considerable degree in keeping with the solution originally proposed by Lohmeyer.[1] Georgi sees the redeemer myth to be not a single myth that existed in a single religion, Gnosticism, but prefers to speak of a 'developing myth';[2] and he finds the particular form of this 'developing myth' that lies behind Phil. ii. 6–11 to be contained almost exclusively in the Sapientia Salomonis. Georgi feels himself pushed to the hypothesis of a 'developing myth' by Käsemann's inability[3] adequately to explain the historical religious background of Phil. ii. 6–11 from the hypothesis of a pre-Christian gnostic redeemer myth alone, and by Ringgren's investigation of the process of hypostatization in Judaism in *Word and Wisdom*.[4] Regarding the place of the Sapientia Salomonis in this development, Georgi says, 'The root and direction of the process of this developing myth can be already recognized...in the Sapientia. Here also one can already establish that the developing myth..., together with the dualistic understanding of the world, belongs to the essential structural components of this new thinking that one calls gnostic.'[5]

The background for Phil. ii. 6–11 is then provided by the Righteous One, i.e. Suffering Servant, who is 'the divine instrument...in the Sapientia'.[6] Georgi sees the figure of the Righteous One in Sapientia as being influenced by the Servant Song of Isa. lii. 13–liii. 12, but as going far beyond the characterization there. This development from the Servant of Isaiah to the Righteous One of Sapientia is twofold; the Righteous One 'loses all individual traits' in Sapientia, thus his fate becomes general and typical, and he becomes a docetic figure, as in Sap. iii. 1–4,

---

[1] Dieter Georgi, 'Der vorpaulinische Hymnus Phil. 2, 6–11', *Zeit und Geschichte. Dankesgabe an Rudolf Bultmann zum 80. Geburtstag*, pp. 263–93.

[2] '*Mythisierung*' and '*Mythisierungsprozess*', *ibid.* pp. 268 f.

[3] In 'Kritische Analyse von Phil. 2, 5–11'.

[4] Georgi, pp. 264, 268.   [5] *Ibid.* p. 269.   [6] *Ibid.* p. 271.

The souls of the righteous are in the hand of God
and no torment will ever touch them.
In the eyes of the foolish they seemed to have died,
and their departure was thought to be an affliction,
and their going from us to be their destruction;
but they are at peace.
For though in the sight of men they were punished,
their hope is full of immortality.

Since the Righteous One elsewhere typifies the existence of the righteous in Sapientia, Georgi attributes to him this docetic suffering and death. Further, the Anthropos who is created in the image of God's eternity (Sap. ii. 23) seems to be identified with the Righteous One.[1] Thus Georgi sees the move in Phil. ii. 6 f. from μορφὴ θεοῦ to μορφὴ δούλου as equivalent to that of the Righteous One; in Phil. ii. 7 'the manner of existence of the slave is assumed—like a garment'.[2]

Both Sap. v and Phil. ii. 8, however, understand the death of the divine figure 'not as end but as turning point'.[3] Thus in Sap. v. 1 one reads, 'Then the Righteous One will stand with great confidence in the presence of those who have afflicted him' (translation mine); and shortly thereafter it is said of the righteous, Sap. v. 16,

They will receive a glorious crown
and a beautiful diadem from the hand of the Lord.

It may therefore be justifiably said of the Righteous One in Sapientia that he was in the form of God, that he took on the form of suffering and death, and that he received (or will receive) an exaltation.

Georgi notes that the statement of pre-existence in Phil. ii. 6 is comparable to statements in Sapientia about Wisdom herself, not about the Righteous One;[4] and this is where Georgi's problems begin. He now assumes an original Jewish hymn structured in *parallelismus membrorum* that has been so reworked from a Christian point of view, to take account of the specific, individual nature of Jesus' death,[5] that it now appears in three-line strophes.[6] This explanation seems to involve mutually

---

[1] *Ibid.* p. 272.   [2] *Ibid.* p. 273.   [3] *Ibid.* p. 274.
[4] *Ibid.* p. 276.   [5] *Ibid.* p. 281.   [6] *Ibid.* pp. 280–9.

contradictory statements, however, explaining the identification in Phil. ii. 6–11 of the pre-existent one with the one who suffers and is exalted. Georgi first seems to suggest that it was Christianity that made this identification in order to explain the Christ event; thus he asks, 'What interest did the Christian community have in speaking also of the pre-existence of the man Jesus?'[1] Yet he guesses that the statement, 'emptied himself', has 'dislodged' an original statement 'about the indwelling of Wisdom in the wise man'.[2] If the original Jewish hymn involved, however, an identification between Sophia and the Righteous One, where and when might such an identification have occurred? Georgi does not discuss this problem. If, on the other hand, the identification was made by Christianity and not by Judaism, how can he speak of a Jewish original which dealt with Sophia and the Righteous One as one entity? 'The carrying over', he says, 'of the motif of pre-existence from Wisdom onto Jesus in Phil. ii. 6 is to show that, where Jesus is concerned, it is a matter of the reality of God and therefore also of the reality of creation, the reality of world and man.'[3] Such generalities, however, seem to be too vague to lend support to Georgi's thesis.

Georgi further thinks that the original parallelism between 'becoming in the likeness of men' and 'being found in fashion like a man' of *v.* 7, which he apparently thinks originally referred to the coming of Sophia to indwell in man, has been separated by the Christian interpretation (which changed the hymn into three-line strophes), so that the singular εὑρεθεὶς ὡς ἄνθρωπος now refers specifically and strictly to the single event of incarnation and ('he humbled himself') self-sacrifice of Christ.[4] One must further object, however, that the *parallelismus membrorum* of Phil. ii. 6–8 is still sufficiently clear not to necessitate an explanation of an original but now distorted *parallelismus membrorum*.

One may raise the question, why indeed it is necessary to suppose a Jewish original for this hymn at all. Could it not be simply a Christian composition, in which the author has drawn upon certain concepts—perhaps combining them but perhaps finding them already combined—to explain the Christ event?

---

[1] *Ibid.* p. 276.   [2] *Ibid.* p. 280.
[3] *Ibid.* p. 278.   [4] *Ibid.* p. 282.

Would it not in fact solve more problems to suppose at least a somewhat more general—or more diverse—background for this hymn than the Sapientia Salomonis alone, which seems to be the thing that has driven Georgi into the problem of finding some solution, necessarily overly complex and incomplete, of how concepts applied both to Sophia and to the Righteous One in Sapientia come together in this hymn? Precisely Ringgren's work, which Georgi cites favorably as one of the prime factors leading him to his first, theoretical conclusion regarding the modification of the hypothesis of a pre-Christian gnostic redeemer myth, should have helped him to avoid taking only one work as the historical religious background for Phil. ii. 6–11, which then raises as many problems as it solves. When Georgi speaks of a 'developing myth' he is definitely on the right track, but the Sapientia Salomonis has sidetracked him.

Thus the discussion of the historical religious background of this hymn remains the most unsettled of the discussions regarding the various hymns; and it is the tantalizing yet vague relationship the passage seems to have to Isa. lii. 13–liii. 12 that is the unsettling factor. Georgi has probably indicated the most adequate solution with his 'developing myth'. If concepts related to Sophia, Logos, and, as was suggested by Héring's study, Anthropos can intermingle and move toward the concepts expressed in the New Testament Christological hymns then there is no reason why the Servant, the Righteous One—to be sure not directly from Isaiah but from the Sapientia Salomonis and Jewish apocalypticism—might not also, having become a divine figure, take up some of the attributes and activities of the other divine figures. If one may still assume, Georgi notwithstanding, that Phil. ii. 6–11, with its incarnation, death, and exaltation, is a Christian product, then one may see the hymn as being what one might expect from an attempt to explain the Christ event by means of this current Jewish myth.

That would not necessarily mean that the hymn actually spoke of the Righteous One. The word δοῦλος in *v.* 7 is most likely to be seen, with Käsemann, as an expression of the redeemer's entering the anti-divine sphere; this would coincide with the formal antithesis between the first and last lines of the first stanza. It might then be that the account of the enthronement led to a certain reliance on the language of Isa. xlv, without the author's thinking of Isa. lii f. The fact that there are so many points of contact between this hymn and the Servant, however, tends to make one think that Georgi was correct in emphasizing the role of the Righteous One in Sapientia as at least a major component in the historical religious background of Phil. ii. 6–11.

CHAPTER 4

COLOSSIANS i. 15–20

A CONVERGENCE OF MOTIFS: MARTIN DIBELIUS

When one next turns to the literature related to the hymn of Col. i. 15–20, one finds oneself once again away from the realm of allusions to the Deutero-Isaianic Servant that so peculiarly characterize the hymn of Phil. ii. 6–11 and clearly in the presence of terminology dealing with cosmic creation and redemption. Yet the two hymns have much in common. Thus, to the extent that this hymn exhibits concepts similar to those in Phil. ii. 6–11, it is itself support on the side of the argument that says that the Christology of Phil. ii. 6–11 cannot be explained merely from the Old Testament.

In his excursus entitled 'The Presentation of Christ as World Soul and World Creator', Martin Dibelius[1] observed that this passage deals with 'a *cosmic* speculation' and 'a *soteriological* conception' that are prior to the 'conceptual world of Paul'.[2] Certain aspects of the cosmic speculation might have stemmed from Stoicism, the *Stufenreihe* (God–World–Man) and the *Allmachtsformel* (τὰ πάντα δι' αὐτοῦ καὶ εἰς αὐτόν).[3] The observation of a parallel with Stoicism is not sufficient, however, for explaining the presence of these elements in the hymn; for Dibelius noted that 'the eschatological relationship comes closer. Then the sense would have to be grasped as in the great Paris magical papyrus...2838: ἐκ σέο γὰρ πάντ' ἐστὶ καὶ εἰς ⟨σ'⟩, αἰών⟨ι⟩ε, πάντα τελευτᾷ'.[4]

---

[1] Dibelius, *An die Kolosser, Epheser, an Philemon* (HNT, 12) (Tübingen, 1953[3]; rev. by Heinrich Greeven), pp. 14–17.

[2] That Paul wrote Colossians is throughout not questioned by Dibelius.

[3] *Ibid.* pp. 13–15. Norden, pp. 249 f., 347 f., had first called attention to the latter of the two. The presence of stoic concepts in the New Testament Christological hymns is in reality most probably to be explained from Wisdom speculation, for Sapientia shows stoic influence throughout. Thus in Sap. xv. 1 God is described as διοικῶν τὰ πάντα. Cf. Ziener, p. 140.

[4] Dibelius, *An die Kolosser*, pp. 13 f. Cf. also Robinson, 'A Formal Analysis', who observes that, although Col. i. 16*c* can be recognized as a stoic *Allmachtsformel*, the other lines in the hymn exhibit 'less philosophical and

Dibelius further pointed to the place of the primal Man in Philo's thought, observing that 'with Philo...the cosmological speculation is linked to a religious concept'.[1] Here, the old idea that the world is the son of God has been divided, so that there are two sons, the κόσμος νοητός and the κόσμος αἰσθητός.[2] Of the older son it can be said that 'he is the organ of God's work of creation (de Migratione Abrahami 6), mediator, and revealer of God (Deus imm. 138), and...καὶ γὰρ ἀρχὴ καὶ ὄνομα θεοῦ καὶ ὁ κατ' εἰκόνα ἄνθρωπος καὶ ὁ ὁρῶν, Ἰσραήλ, προσαγορεύεται (de Conf. Ling. 146).'[3]

The problem of the immediate historical religious background of Col. i. 15–20 is still posed, however, by the question, 'to what extent the All can already have had its existence in Christ if he must yet, according to i. 20, "reconcile" the All'.[4] It is this paradoxical situation that finally points to Gnosticism, since in Gnosticism the concept of the All as 'a giant human being'[5] is combined with that of a cosmic redeemer. 'Thus

more religious categories'. Dibelius further observed that similar statements about the All are to be found in the pantheism of Hermetic literature, as in Corp. Herm. v. 10, πάντα δὲ ἐν σοί, πάντα ἀπὸ σοῦ.

[1] Ibid. p. 15.

[2] Quod Deus immutabilis sit 31. Cf. further de Opificio 20 ff., where Philo discusses the ἀνὴρ ἀρχιτεκτονικός who bears in his ψυχή the τύποι of the νοητὴ πόλις. καθάπερ οὖν ἡ ἐν τῷ ἀρχιτεκτονικῷ προδιατυπωθεῖσα πόλις χώραν ἐκτὸς οὐκ εἶχεν, ἀλλ' ἐνεσφράγιστο τῇ τοῦ τεχνίτου ψυχῇ, τὸν αὐτὸν τρόπον οὐδ' ὁ ἐκ τῶν ἰδεῶν κόσμος ἄλλον ἂν ἔχοι τόπον ἢ τὸν θεῖον λόγον τὸν ταῦτα διακοσμήσαντα...εἰ δέ τις ἐθελήσειε γυμνοτέροις χρήσασθαι τοῖς ὀνόμασιν, οὐδὲν ἂν ἕτερον εἴποι τὸν νοητὸν κόσμον εἶναι ἢ θεοῦ λόγον ἤδη κοσμοποιοῦντος· οὐδὲ γὰρ ἡ νοητὴ πόλις ἕτερόν τί ἐστιν ἢ ὁ τοῦ ἀρχιτέκτονος λογισμὸς ἤδη τὴν πόλιν κτίζειν διανοουμένου...εἰ δὲ τὸ μέρος εἰκὼν εἰκόνος [δῆλον ὅτι] καὶ τὸ ὅλον εἶδος, σύμπας οὗτος ὁ αἰσθητὸς κόσμος, εἰ μείζων τῆς ἀνθρωπίνης ἐστίν, μίμημα θείας εἰκόνος, δῆλον ὅτι καὶ ἡ ἀρχέτυπος σφραγίς, ὅν φαμεν νοητὸν εἶναι κόσμον, αὐτὸς ἂν εἴη [τὸ παράδειγμα, ἀρχέτυπος ἰδέα τῶν ἰδεῶν] ὁ θεοῦ λόγος. The λόγος is then called in de Confusione Linguarum 146 πρωτόγονος and τῶν ἀγγέλων πρεσβύτατος.

[3] Norden, Die Geburt des Kindes. Geschichte einer religiösen Idee (Studien der Bibliothek Warburg, 3) (Leipzig, 1924), p. 99, had also discussed the relation of these two sons to the hymn of John i. In Deus imm. 31 the υἱὸς νοητός is the λόγος who stayed with God (παρ' ἑαυτῷ καταμένειν διενοήθη), but τὸν μόνον καὶ ἀγαπητὸν αἰσθητὸν υἱὸν ἀπεκύησε τόνδε τὸν κόσμον. Thus Norden concluded that the prologue of John combined the concepts of these two sons.   [4] Dibelius, An die Kolosser, p. 14.

[5] Cf. Hippolytus, Refutatio Omnium Haeresium viii. 12, Μονόϊμος...λέγει ἄνθρωπον εἶναι τὸ πᾶν...

there would immediately follow a connection between the two parts of [the hymn]; for the firstborn of all creatures is the primal Man, but the firstborn of the dead is the "redeemed redeemer".' It was therefore in Iranian religion that Dibelius found the nearest parallel to Col. i. 15–20. In the Mandaean literature, the divine messenger *Manda dHaije* combines cosmological and soteriological functions, just as the redeemer here in Col. i. 15–20; and in the Mandaean literature 'what is to be redeemed appears as the image of the redeemer'. Thus the 'Man' says to *Mānā* in *Ginzā* 461, 31 f., 'You are my image, I wish to exalt you and preserve you in my raiment'. Even this parallel, however, is not taken to be the sole milieu from which Col. i. 15–20 is to be understood; rather, Dibelius argued, 'Paul sees his Christ in the place of the κόσμος of the Hermetic writings, the κόσμος νοητός-λόγος of Philo, and the primal Man of the "Iranian" texts.'[1]

Quite in keeping, now, with what has already been seen to be the case with regard to the prologue of John and Phil. ii. 6–11, Dibelius thought that Hellenistic Judaism had already laid the ground for the similarity between the Christian concept of the redeemer found in Col. i. 15–20 and the other concepts he had shown to be related 'perhaps less by the identifying of the "Man" with the Messiah, but rather with "Wisdom"'. Thus Col. i. 15 ff. is seen to be like a praise of Wisdom.[2] Prov. viii.

[1] Dibelius, *An die Kolosser*, p. 16. The contrary opinion of Manson, p. 186, that the reference to the Son in Col. i. 13 rules out any influence from Iranian mythology in the hymn (Manson gives *vv.* 13–17), falls, of course, on the realization that *vv.* 15–20 are by and large a quotation. In spite of his negative conclusions, Manson gives a full and fairly sympathetic treatment of the question of Iranian influence on Christianity in the section pp. 174–90. A very good treatment of the texts related to the myth of the Man is given by J. M. Creed, 'The Heavenly Man', *JTS*, vol. xxvi (1925), pp. 113–36. Creed was primarily interested in the origin of the Son of man concept in apocalyptic Judaism, which does not concern us here.

[2] *Ibid.* p. 16. Cf. further Davies, *Paul and Rabbinic Judaism*, pp. 150–2. It has already been observed in ch. 2 that the relation of Sophia to these hymns is not merely that of the influence of Sophia speculation on, for example, the concept of the Logos or Anthropos. What seems rather to have been the case was a coordinate growth of ideas relating to various hypostases. Thus Philo's remark in *de Conf. Ling.* 146, quoted above, is a true reflection of the situation with regard to the hypostases of divine qualities (and the growth of the idea of a divine Man) in that it indicates that what was implied when one referred to Anthropos or Logos or Sophia was in any case

22–5, for example, seemed to Dibelius to deal with 'what Paul names πρωτότοκος πάσης κτίσεως'.[1] Both Ode Sol. xxxiii and Enoch xlviii. 2, 3, and 6, where the Son of man is described with terms elsewhere applied to Sophia, were further evidence to Dibelius that the concepts associated with Sophia could be applied to other beings.[2]

To see pre-Christian Judaism as the place where the ground was laid for the ideas expressed in Col. i. 15–20 is doubtless correct, and Dibelius was probably very close to the truth when he supposed that already prior to Christianity the Sophia and the primal Man-redeemer had somehow blended into one figure. The situation that has come to light, however, in the discussion of the prologue of John and of Phil. ii. 6–11 would tend to make one think that the situation was more complex than Dibelius assumed; and, indeed, some of the passages he cites, particularly from Philo, attest such a complex situation. It is not to be overlooked that none of the figures he names quite fills the whole role of the redeemer in Col. i. 15–20. Thus to speak of a 'developing myth' would seem to be most accurate, the related myths expressed in the New Testament Christological hymns representing a later stage of the development than Wisdom literature or the Iranian myth of the primal Man-redeemer. Dibelius was unable to explain where, when, and under what circumstances the Iranian myth of the primal Man-redeemer might have come into pre-Christian Judaism; and it further still remains unclear whether the later stage of the

the same (or quite similar). This indefinite state with regard to hypostatization was noticed as long ago as 1914 by Hans Windisch. He termed this phenomenon 'that many-figured hypostasis of Hellenistic syncretism... which is designated now as Wisdom, now as Spirit of God, now as Logos, now as world soul' (Windisch, p. 221).

[1] Similarly, Windisch (p. 222) saw this phrase as referring to the same general being as Sir. i. 4, προτέρα πάντων ἔκτισται σοφία, Sir. i. 9, κύριος αὐτὸς ἔκτισεν αὐτὴν [sc. Σοφίαν], and Sir. xxiv. 9, πρὸ τοῦ αἰῶνος ἀπ' ἀρχῆς ἔκτισέν με. Particularly, the word εἰκών could be used in Col. i. 15 in a way similar to Sap. vii. 26, εἰκὼν τῆς ἀγαθότητος αὐτοῦ, yet also perhaps 'inspired by Gen. i. 26 f.' (ibid. p. 223). The 'bringing together of Wisdom with the stoic world spirit or world soul' in Sap. vii. 22 ff. Windisch took to be the explanation of the inclusion of the stoic Allmachtsformel in Col. i. 17.
[2] Dibelius, An die Kolosser, p. 17; cf. also James Muilenburg, 'The Son of Man in Daniel and the Ethiopic Apocalypse of Enoch', JBL, vol. LXXIX (1960), pp. 208 f.

'developing myth' was reached already prior to Christianity, or whether the Christ event provided the magnet which drew the various elements together.

THE GNOSTIC REDEEMER AS A JEWISH FIGURE:
ERNST KÄSEMANN

The fact that only eight of the 112 words in *vv.* 15–20 need be removed in order to remove all specifically Christian elements from the text leads Ernst Käsemann to the conclusion that the present hymn is pre-Christian.[1] What remains after removing these eight words is 'gnostic terminology...in which the redeemer, as preparer of the way and leader of those who are his, knocks a breach in the sphere of the dead. In this way creation and re-creation are constitutively bound together in the myth of the primal Man who is the redeemer.' Käsemann thinks that 'the super-historic and metaphysical drama of the gnostic redeemer' is present here, as in Phil. ii. 6–11, and he agrees with Dibelius that in this hymn 'primal Man and Sophia, i.e. Logos speculation are bound up together'.[2] Whereas originally in Jewish thought Adam and only Adam possessed 'the quality of being in the image of God', for Philo, Plutarch, and the *Corpus Hermeticum* 'the cosmos counts as the firstborn and image of God and thus as the Son of God and δεύτερος θεός. From this point it was possible for Hellenistic Judaism to take over the [same] predicate for Sophia and Logos, insofar as the first is also "firstborn" and, as πάρεδρος, is also in fact δεύτερος θεός.' When, then, in Philo 'the doctrine of Sophia or Logos and of primal Man blend together into each other, the *eikon* concept can appear directly as a uniting bond between the two'.[3]

It is this background that explains for Käsemann why the 'Microcosmos...Macro-Anthropos' concept is connected with soteriology in this hymn, for while 'the world...[is] Adam's

---

[1] Käsemann, 'Eine urchristliche Taufliturgie', p. 39.

[2] *Ibid.* p. 40.

[3] *Ibid.* p. 41. Thus the explanation Käsemann gives for the historical religious background of this hymn is much nearer the situation that is emerging here into clarity—that of a 'developing myth' (Georgi)—than the explanation he gave, originally a year later, for the historical religious background of Phil. ii. 6–11.

body, he its soul or head', it is Sophia who has a soteriological function in Judaism (Prov. viii. 34; Sap. vii. 24 ff.; Ode Sol. xxxiii).[1] Thus it is Käsemann's view that concepts related to Adam and Sophia are united in Col. i. 15–20 with the concept of the 'Cosmocrator, in whose honor Phil. ii. 11 speaks of the general subjugation, Heb. i. 6 ff. of the genuflection of the powers, and I Tim. iii. 16 of the "believed in the world"...The restituted creation is his work. Insofar as the latter constitutes his body from now on, he himself is the "redeemed redeemer".'[2]

Käsemann has thus here given an interpretation of the pre-Christian gnostic redeemer that again reveals the varied nature of this 'figure'; for whereas Bultmann had apparently thought of the concept of this redeemer as influencing the concepts of Sophia, Anthropos, and Logos, Käsemann sees these as being *ingredients that come together to make up the gnostic redeemer*. The gnostic redeemer would thus, on this view, have arisen within Judaism (so also Georgi). Thus Käsemann's explanation has the effect of substantiating the view that has been emerging in the course of the discussion of the historical religious background of these several hymns. This view is that, when one takes what is common to the figures of Logos, Anthropos, Sophia, the Christ of the New Testament Christological hymns, and other similar redeemer figures, one has the gnostic redeemer; but that this does not imply that there ever was any such figure, rather that the various divine figures began in pre-Christian Judaism to take on similar redemptive aspects as the result of a developing mythical understanding, and that the New Testament Christological hymns represent a further stage in that process. Whether Käsemann is correct in thinking that just such a mythical scheme as is presented here was present already in pre-Christian Judaism still remains, however, not entirely clear.

IMAGE: F.-W. ELTESTER

Käsemann had suggested that the concept of the 'image' was the focal point around which the concepts related to the several divine beings clustered and intermingled.[3] It was the work of F.-W. Eltester to investigate this possibility.[4] Eltester found that

---

[1] *Ibid.* p. 42.   [2] *Ibid.* p. 43.   [3] Above, p. 79.
[4] F.-W. Eltester, *Eikon im Neuen Testament* (BZNW, 23) (Berlin, 1958).

in Hellenistic Judaism 'the Logos as *eikon* of God represents a divine being who takes a prominent position over against all other created beings: ὁ δὲ...λόγος θεῖος...αὐτὸς εἰκὼν ὑπάρχων θεοῦ, τῶν νοητῶν ἅπαξ ἁπάντων ὁ πρεσβύτατος, ὁ ἐγγυτάτω...'.[1] Thus Eltester again demonstrates what has already here become obvious, that the Logos is for Philo 'mediator of creation', and 'the hypostatized perceptibility of God'.[2] A similar situation of course also exists with regard to Anthropos in *de Conf. Ling.* 62–4; 'The Anthropos is here a divine being, the eldest Son of God, and plays a role as mediator of creation.' Thus he is identified with the Logos, 'the Man of God (ἄνθρωπος θεοῦ), who is himself, as the Logos of the Eternal One, immortal'.[3] Observing that Sophia is God's *eikon* in Sap. vii. 26, Eltester thus rightly concludes, 'Logos and Anthropos can thus interchange in Philo, as can also Logos and Sophia in a similar manner'; hence the equating of the Logos with ἀρχή, ὄνομα, and ἄνθρωπος in *de Conf. Ling.* 146.[4]

In the dualistic pessimistic group of the Hermetic tractates, Eltester again finds a concept similar to that of Philo and Col. i. 15–20 in which Anthropos is the *eikon* of the godhead (in this case *Nous*) in the sense of an essential similarity or identity. *Corp. Herm.* i. 12: ὁ δὲ πάντων πατὴρ ὁ Νοῦς, ὢν ζωὴ καὶ φῶς,[5] ἀπεκύησεν Ἄνθρωπον αὐτῷ ἴσον, οὗ ἠράσθη ὡς ἰδίου τόκου. Eltester elaborates: 'As the Father, so also is the Anthropos φῶς and ζωή; both have the same "essence"; just as the Father is called Νοῦς, the Man is called ἔννους [i. 18].'[6]

Eltester thus ascribes to the '*eikon* predication of the Logos' in Hellenistic Judaism two roots that are nearly the same as the two sources Dibelius suggested for Col. i. 15–20. One is 'in the doctrine of Sophia...The second root lies in the doctrine of the cosmic Anthropos.'[7] This is to be seen specifically, then, in

---

[1] *Ibid.* p. 35; Philo *de Fuga et Inv.* 101.

[2] F.-W. Eltester, pp. 35–7; cf. *de Opificio* 19, *Leg. Alleg.* iii. 99.

[3] F.-W. Eltester, p. 39; Philo *de Conf. Ling.* 41.

[4] Above, p. 76.

[5] Cf. John i. 4!   [6] F.-W. Eltester, p. 81.

[7] *Ibid.* p. 120. Thus Eltester's explanation, in distinction from that of Dibelius, finds the concept of the Man here in Judaism itself and not in Iranian religion.

Here should be mentioned two very interesting works dealing with the relation of the concept of the 'image' to Gnosticism. The first is that of

Col. i. 15–20. 'From her [sc. Sophia], all the features in vv. 15–18a can be understood up to the assertion in v. 18a; one cannot say of the Sophia, she is the head of the body. Here the figure of the Aeon–primal Man comes to light.'[1] Eltester then agrees with Käsemann that 'Hellenistic Judaism has already fused together the figures of Wisdom and primal Man; Philo and the hymn used by the author of Colossians go back in this respect to Hellenistic Judaism'.[2]

Eltester supports this conclusion further by showing parallels among Col. i. 15 ff., the Philonic Logos, the Aeon of *Corp. Herm.* xi, and the Cosmos of *Corp. Herm.* xii.[3] Eltester summarizes:

In Hellenistic Judaism, for which Philo serves as our source, an intermediate being, in whom the figure of Sophia and the figure of Anthropos flow together, bears the designation εἰκὼν τοῦ θεοῦ. This intermediate being participates in the creating and sustaining of the world. It represents the entirety of the world insofar as the world is its body, but it transcends the world as head. The hymn in Col. i. 15 ff. carries over such a presentation onto Christ, whereby the stoic τὰ πάντα formula is made use of, and whereby in addition gnostic motifs show their influence.[4] This presentation belongs in the large

Jakob Jervell (*Imago Dei*), the other is by Hans-Martin Schenke (*Der Gott 'Mensch' in der Gnosis* (Göttingen, 1962)). Both of these authors attempt to distinguish between Jewish and gnostic usage of the 'image' concept, and both attribute the presence of that concept in both Judaism and Gnosticism to interpretation of Gen. i. 26 f. Since the image is spoken of in the context of creation in Col. i. 15 f., Jervell (pp. 200 f.) takes the hymn to be Christian from a Jewish background; and Schenke (p. 122) tries to show a difference between Gnosticism's use of Gen. i. 26 f. and Philo's use of the passage— an attempt which must be considered altogether abortive. Even if Gen. i. 26 f. could be shown to be the origin of the 'image' concept in Hellenism (something which Eltester's work makes impossible), one would have to ask whether the fact that Gnostics were interested in Genesis would not point to a relation between Jews and Gnostics, even to Jewish Gnostics.

[1] F.-W. Eltester, p. 140. Regarding this expression, Schlier, 'κεφαλή, ἀνακεφαλαιόομαι', *TDNT*, vol. iii, ed. Gerhard Kittel, trans. and ed. Geoffrey W. Bromiley (Grand Rapids, Michigan, 1965), p. 681, observed that 'Christ is not merely the Redeemer; He is also the First Man. These are not alongside one another. In the Redeemer the First Man is at work.'

[2] F.-W. Eltester, p. 140.

[3] *Ibid.* pp. 140 f.; cf. the table on pp. 84–5, reprinted here by permission.

[4] Yet it has already been seen that stoic ideas were already connected with Sophia in Sapientia (above, p. 75 n. 3). The need to refer to 'gnostic motifs' shows, regrettably, that Eltester has brought us not much farther than the solution offered by Dibelius.

scope of the cosmological speculation of Hellenism; the Hermetic Aeon is particularly to be cited as parallel. Thus in the Jewish as in the heathen environment of Colossians a cosmic being bears the designation 'image of God'.[1]

Eltester further relates the Colossians hymn to the hymn in the prologue of John: 'The author of the Gospel of John evidently avoids the term *eikon* altogether, perhaps because it was too cosmologically loaded for him.' Eltester understands this to be merely a formal discrepancy, however, and not a material one, for he takes the concept of the Logos in John i to be the same as that of the redeemer of Col. i. 15 ff.[2]

Eltester's work has thus considerably strengthened Dibelius' solution of the problem of the historical religious background of Col. i. 15–20 by showing still more plainly the relation of *vv.* 15–18 to pre-Christian Judaism. In so doing, he has brought a necessary correction to Dibelius' position by showing that one must not limit the parallels to these verses to the Sophia herself, since both in Philo and in the *Corpus Hermeticum* a comparable figure is also the head of the body. Eltester has consequently come nearer than Dibelius to explaining the whole conceptuality of this hymn from pre-Christian Judaism; but he still has not done so entirely, since there remains the problem of the reconciliation.[3] This remains, then, the central problem. Was the Christ event the focal point that brought together concepts

[1] F.-W. Eltester, p. 147. Also Reitzenstein, *Zwei religionsgeschichtliche Fragen*, p. 112, thought in terms of an abstract idea lying equally behind Sophia, Logos, and Nomos. The mythical beings '*grow up from the same root and constantly merge into one another*. As λόγος and νόμος are many times compared to each other, so both with our author [*sc.* of Sapientia] and with Sirach σοφία (γνῶσις) and νόμος.'

[2] F.-W. Eltester, p. 152. Thus the Logos is called κεφαλὴ τοῦ κόσμου (cf. Col. i. 18!) in Philo *Quaest. in Exodum* ii. 117.

[3] Scroggs, pp. 55 f., has shown how some rabbinic texts, engaged in Adamic speculation, anticipated the *Endzeit* of Adam in terms of his *Urzeit* and related this primarily to soteriology. Scroggs notes, 'An anthropological concern underlies Adamic mythology, a concern which drives the theologians to depict what will be man's future on the basis of God's "past", His perfect intent in creation' (*ibid.* p. 56). It is possible that such Adamic speculation paved the way for the connection made in Col. i. 15–20. Probably no more than that. Deichgräber, pp. 149, 152 f., expresses himself strongly in favor of F.-W. Eltester's position.

Christ (Col. i. 15 ff.)	The Philonic Logos	The Aeon of Corp. Herm. xi	The Cosmos of Corp. Herm. xii
v. 15 a εἰκὼν τοῦ θεοῦ	de Fuga et Inv. 101 εἰκὼν ὑπάρχων θεοῦ	εἰκὼν τοῦ θεοῦ 15	ὁ μέγας θεὸς καὶ τοῦ μεί- ζονος εἰκών 15
v. 15 b πρω- τότοκος πάσης κτίσεως; cf. v. 17 a αὐτός ἐστι πρὸ πάν- των	πρωτόγονος de Conf. Ling. 146; ὁ μὲν πρεσβύτατος τοῦ ὄντος de Fuga et Inv. 101; τῶν νοη- τῶν ἅπαξ ἁ- πάντων πρεσ- βύτατος de Fuga et Inv. 110		
v. 16 a ἐν αὐτῷ ἐκτίσθη τὰ πάντα	καθάπερ οὖν ἡ ἐν τῷ ἀρχι- τεκτονικῷ προδιατυπω- θεῖσα πόλις χώραν ἐκτὸς οὐκ εἶχεν, ἀλλ' ἐνε- σφράγιστο τῇ τοῦ τεχνικοῦ ψυχῇ, τὸν αὐ- τὸν τρόπον οὐδ' ὁ ἐκ τῶν ἰδεῶν κόσμος ἄλλον ἂν ἔχοι τόπον ἢ τὸν θεῖον λόγον de Opificio 20ᵃ	ὁ αἰὼν δὲ τὸν κόσμον [sc. ποιεῖ] 2 ὁ δὲ κόσμος ἐν τῷ αἰῶνι 2	τὰ ἐν αὐτῷ [sc. τῷ κόσ- μῳ] 16 οὐδ' ἔστιν ἐν τούτῳ [sc. τῷ κόσμῳ]... οὔτε τοῦ παν- τὸς οὔτε τῶν κατὰ μέρος ὃ οὐχὶ ζῇ
v. 16 b τὰ πάντα δι' αὐ- τοῦ ... ἔκ- τισται	ὁ λόγος δι' οὗ πᾶς ὁ κόσ- μος ἐδημιουρ- γεῖτο de Specialibus Legibus i. 81; ὁ λόγος δι' οὗ ὁ κόσμος κατεσκευάσθη de Cherub. 127	ὁ αἰὼν δὲ τὸν κόσμον [sc. ποιεῖ] 2 πάντα δὲ ταῦ- τα διὰ τοῦ αἰῶνος 4	

Christ (Col. i. 15 ff.)	The Philonic Logos	The Aeon of Corp. Herm. xi	The Cosmos of Corp. Herm. xii
v. 16b τὰ πάν-τα...εἰς αὐτὸν ἔκτισ-ται^b v. 17b τὰ πάν-τα ἐν αὐτῷ συνέστηκε	ἐνδύεται δ' ὁ μὲν πρεσβύτα-τος τοῦ ὄντος ὡς ἐσθῆτα τὸν κόσμον de Fuga et Inv. 110; δεσμὸς ἁπάντων... συνέχει τὰ μέρη πάντα de Fuga et Inv. 112	ὁ δὲ κόσμος ἐν τῷ αἰῶνι 2 συνέχει τοῦ-τον [sc. τὸν κόσμον] ὁ αἰών 4	πῶς ἂν οὖν δύναιτο, ὦ τέκνον, ἐν τῷ θεῷ, ἐν τῇ τοῦ παντὸς εἰκόνι, ἐν τῷ τῆς ζωῆς πλη-ρώματι (i.e. in the cosmos) νεκρὰ εἶναι; 16 οὐκ ἀποθνή-σκει οὖν... τὰ ἐν αὐτῷ ζῷα, ὄντα αὐ-τοῦ μέρη 16
v. 18a κεφαλὴ τοῦ σώματος	The head of all things is the eternal Logos of the eternal God, under which, as if it were feet or limbs, is placed the whole world Quaestiones et Solutiones in Exodum ii. 117^c	τοῦ δὲ κόσμου [sc. ψυχὴ] ὁ αἰών 5 τὸ δὲ πᾶν τοῦ-το τὸ σῶμα, ἐν ᾧ τὰ πάντα ἐστὶ σώματα, ψυχὴ πλήρης τοῦ νοῦ καὶ τοῦ Θεοῦ [i.e. the Aeon] ἐν-τὸς μὲν αὐτὸ πληροῖ ἐκτὸς δὲ περιλαμ-βάνει, ζωο-ποιοῦσα τὸ πᾶν 4	

a F.-W. Eltester, p. 140 n. 81: 'The passage from Philo is to be cited only as a formal parallel to Col. i. 16a. A material parallel is not present, since Philo intends only the world of ideas, Col. i. 15 ff., on the other hand, the All inclusive of the material world.'

b Eltester notes that this *Allmachtsformel* has no exact parallel with the Philonic Logos or with the Hermetic Aeon (*ibid.* p. 146). Yet, to the extent that these figures, as well as that of Christ in Col. i. 15–20, are related to the concept of Sophia, this should present no problem; for Sapientia shows strong stoic influence and comes very close to the *Allmachtsformel* when it is said of Sophia in vii. 24 that she διήκει δὲ καὶ χωρεῖ διὰ πάντων.

c Schlier, on the other hand, 'κεφαλή', p. 677, sees the concept of the Logos as head of the Cosmos in Philo, particularly the commentary on Exodus, as being stoic in the sense of a διοικητής rather than gnostic in the sense of a σωτήρ.

85

related to the various divine figures in Judaism with the idea of a cosmic reconciliation? Had the Jewish Wisdom-like figures already merged with a cosmic redeemer in some as yet undetected area of pre-Christian Judaism? If this should prove to be the case, would that resulting figure then be the gnostic redeemer, or would the prior cosmic redeemer be he? Probably the former; yet it still cannot be demonstrated entirely satisfactorily that such a merger did occur prior to Christianity, and that the Christ event was not in fact the focal point in this merger.[1]

Since the now rather well-attested hypothesis of a 'process of developing myth' in pre-Christian Judaism goes far toward explaining how such concepts as are found in the New Testament Christological hymns could be predicated of Jesus, one might simply assume that the Christ event provided one segment of Judaism, primitive Christianity, with the motif that effected a move to a next stage in this development, the stage in which a cosmic reconciliation was attributed to the redeemer figure.[2] That would surely be an answer. One might even argue

[1] If in the case of Phil. ii. 6–11 it could be reasonably suggested that the Righteous One of Sapientia and of apocalyptic literature provided the motif of the exaltation, still that figure could hardly be related to the cosmic reconciliation, the new creation of Col. i. 18*b*–20. Precisely here, however, is seen the problem of that explanation of Phil. ii. 9–11, since the exaltation of the Righteous One in Judaism remains a vindication, whereas in Phil. ii. 9–11 there is a cosmic victory.

[2] This is basically the solution offered by Eduard Schweizer, who ('Die Kirche als Leib Christi in den paulinischen Antilegomena', cols 243 f.) understands the first part of the hymn, including the phrase 'head of the body', to be rooted in pre-Christian Judaism (in reliance on F.-W. Eltester), the second stanza to be 'originally Christian'. Cf. further the extensive and competent support given this explanation by Harald Hegermann, *Die Vorstellung vom Schöpfungsmittler im hellenistischen Judentum und Urchristentum* (Texte und Untersuchungen zur Geschichte der altchristlichen Literatur, 82) (Berlin, 1961), pp. 93–137. Hegermann concludes concisely (*ibid.* p. 132): 'The hymn of Col. i stands within the context of an old and widespread Christological conception of Hellenistic Christianity prior to and contemporary with Paul, which carried over the primitive kerygma of the resurrection of the crucified Messiah Jesus and his exaltation to eschatological lord over the world into the conceptuality of Hellenistic-Jewish circles. This transposition availed itself of combinations already present.' Such a conclusion certainly lies close; but we hope to demonstrate in Part 3 that some newly discovered texts, as well as a new reading of others that have been

that the view that the reconciliation had already taken place or was now in the process of being realized—as in I Cor. xv. 20–4—could *only* be Christian. That such a view is credible but not necessary will be seen in Part 3.

around awhile, establishes a likely milieu in Hellenistic Judaism, the conceptuality of which is closer to the conceptuality of these hymns than is envisioned by Eltester, Schweizer, and Hegermann.

CHAPTER 5

THE SHORTER PASSAGES

EPHESIANS ii. 14–16

Heinrich Schlier, in his *Habilitationsschrift* of 1928,[1] gave the fullest evidence that has been given on the side of the gnostic background of this passage. Schlier found the concept of the redeemer who destroys the hostile wall (or fortress, or wall of fire, or iron wall) between the godhead and those who are to be redeemed to be well attested in the Mandaean literature. In the Mandaean Liturgy, p. 201, the Man who springs from Tibil knocks a cleft in the house in which the sad ones await him; in the Left Ginza, 533 f., the same Man knocks a cleft in the fortress which holds the sad ones; and in the Left Ginza, 551, 1 ff., the Man says,

> In this wall, the iron wall,
> I will knock a breach for you.[2]

When language highly similar to that used in Eph. ii. 14 then turns up in Ign. *Tral.* ix. 4 and the Acts of Thaddeus (Eusebius, *Historia Ecclesiastica* i. 13, 20)—in both cases, however, linked with a statement about the *descensus ad inferos*—Schlier concluded that this could not be the result of reliance on Eph. ii. 14; therefore, the Mandaean literature, Eph. ii. 14, and the two occurrences in other Christian writings must rely on a common myth.[3]

The argument Schlier gave, which had originally been formulated by Reitzenstein, for the existence of a myth of a divine Man (Anthropos) who, as the act of redemption, incorporated the redeemed so that they became together a macro-anthropos,[4] is today so generally known that it hardly needs a summary repetition here. One should note at least, however, a Manichaean 'song', which extols,

[1] Schlier, *Christus und die Kirche im Epheserbrief.*
[2] *Ibid.* pp. 20 f.
[3] *Ibid.* p. 23.
[4] *Ibid.* pp. 27–37, 'Der himmlische Anthropos'.

We praise and extol and glorify greatly
Srōš (h)rōē,
the perfect man,
the adamantine appearing pillar
that bears the worlds
and fills the All.[1]

Schlier rightly observed that, if one cannot argue, because of the lateness of the Mandaean and Manichaean texts, that Manichaeism influenced Ephesians at this point, neither may the reverse be argued, since 'the Manichaean concepts are too much imbedded in other mythological concepts, and so closely connected to them' that it is not possible to argue for direct influence from Ephesians. One must rather again postulate a common mythical background.[2] The historical religious situation which might have provided the possibility for such a common background was not, however, discussed.

Schlier did not at first entertain the possibility of a quotation in Eph. ii. 14–18, although he agreed with the current observation that it was an excursus.[3] This led him, of course, to see the whole of the passage as being the author's version of the underlying myth.[4] In his commentary on Ephesians, however,[5] he accepts the thesis of Schille, though with reservation,[6] that a quoted hymn or hymn fragment is present here. This leads him now to speak of a 'reinterpreted text'.[7] More important for our investigation, he now sees the original text—and this is in keeping with what has become obvious regarding the 'developing myth' lying behind the New Testament Christological hymns—to have arisen in 'gnosticizing Judaism'. In order to explain the 'wall', one must 'distinguish three concepts in the background, whose confluence presents...a concrete example for the gnosticizing of Jewish tradition'.[8] That the Jew is set off from the rest of mankind by a wall is represented for Schlier

---

[1] *Ibid.* p. 29.   [2] *Ibid.* p. 31.
[3] Cf. Dibelius, *An die Kolosser*, p. 69.
[4] This view was expressed even more strongly in his later article, 'Die Kirche nach dem Brief an die Epheser', *Die Kirche im Epherserbrief*, by Schlier and Viktor Warnach (Beiträge zur Kontroverstheologie, 1) (Münster-Westfalen, 1949), p. 84.
[5] Schlier, *Der Brief an die Epheser* (Düsseldorf, 1957); the 3rd edn (1962) is cited here.
[6] *Ibid.* p. 123.   [7] *Ibid.* p. 127.   [8] *Ibid.* p. 128.

in the Dead Sea Scrolls,[1] whereas I Enoch xiv. 9 refers to a heavenly wall that separates the heavenly from the earthly sphere; and an allusion in rabbinic literature to the serpent's breaking through the wall makes it certain for Schlier that the concept of a wall at once between Jew and gentile (the Torah) and between man and God was present in pre-Christian Judaism. It is this view, then, that is connected to the previously explained myth of the heavenly redeemer who breaks down the wall.

Similarly, the 'enmity' is now seen in terms of the Ascension of Isaiah vii. 9 ff., where the visionary sees a battle in heaven which has its counterpart on earth;[2] and the background for the 'new Man' is now altered to 'Jewish Adam speculation, influenced by the Oriental, gnostic primal Man–redeemer myth'.[3] Schlier's primary evidence here is Philo.

In spite of the fact that Schlier's historical religious interpretation of this passage has, between 1930 and 1957, moved in the right direction in that he now takes pre-Christian Judaism far more into account, his later explanation is in several respects less satisfactory than his earlier one. Not only are his parallels from Jewish literature less numerous and less clearly parallel, but he has failed to take into account the full range of pre-Christian Jewish mythology. Most of all, he has not seen the extent of the implications involved in accepting the quoted character of Eph. ii. 14–16. Assuming that Ephesians was written from a Jewish Christian point of view as an attempt to reconcile Jewish and gentile Christians—a view which Schlier holds, though now asserting Pauline authorship for the letter—one might readily suppose that the words 'to God' in *v.* 16 were *also* added by the author of the letter. If these words were not original, however, then the hymn would lose the concept of the wall which divides in two ways, between Jew and gentile and between man and God, the element on which Schlier lays so

---

[1] Schlier cites CD vi. 7 ff. and 1QH i. 3. The CD reference follows Charles, and refers to that passage now normally designated as iv. 10 ff. I am unable to find the exact reference intended by 1QH i. 3. The word גָּדֵר appears, in the texts examined in the *Konkordanz zu dem Qumrantexten*, ed. Karl Georg Kuhn (Göttingen, 1960), only at CD iv. 12. חוֹמָה, which also means wall, appears five times in 1QH, but in none of these instances, including CD iv. 12, does the wall function to separate Jews from others.

[2] Schlier, *Der Brief an die Epheser*, p. 129.   [3] *Ibid.* p. 92.

much emphasis; and that which ties it to pre-Christian Judaism would thereby be lost. Since the words 'to God' are in fact, from the point of view of the author, the key words in the hymn, one may certainly hold it to be possible, even probable, that in the original αὐτῷ or ἑαυτῷ, or perhaps nothing at all, stood here instead. However that may be, Schlier has not succeeded as well in tying this hymn to pre-Christian Judaism as he did in relating it to post-New Testament (but independent) Gnosticism. This is to be expected in view of the fact that it is precisely the cosmic reconciliation half of the myth represented in Col. i. 15–20—and also in Phil. ii. 6–11—that cannot be satisfactorily related to Jewish Wisdom or apocalyptic literature. Had Schlier succeeded in tying this hymn, so closely related to Col. i. 18*b*–20, to pre-Christian Judaism, then the historical religious problem posed by the several hymns would be solved, or nearly so. This attempt, however, must be considered not to have carried.

Petr Pokorný has also expressed his opinion that the background of the gnostic concepts found in Ephesians, particularly in this hymn, must be found in an area of pre-Christian Judaism,[1] where 'a gnostic redeemer figure' arose 'from a pre-Christian encounter between spiritualizing syncretism and the Messiah idea in the Old Testament and Judaism'.[2] To a considerable degree, Pokorný's conclusions appear in arbitrary form—that is, not supported by specific examples. He suggests several parallels from the *Corpus Hermeticum* and from the Preaching of the Naassenes for Eph. ii. 14–16,[3] yet these are not uniformly relevant. That *Corp. Herm.* i. 14[4] provides a parallel to the knocking of a breach in the wall in our passage is obvious, and supportive of Schlier's earlier conclusions; and when Pokorný states that 'the *hapax legomenon* ἀμφότεροι...

---

[1] Petr Pokorný, 'Epheserbrief und gnostische Mysterien', *ZNW*, vol. LIII (1962), pp. 160–94; cf. further Pokorný, *Der Epheserbrief und die Gnosis. Die Bedeutung des Haupt-Glieder-Gedankens in der entstehenden Kirche* (Berlin, 1965), pp. 114 f.

[2] *Ibid.* p. 163. Cf. further Walter Schmithals, *Die Gnosis in Korinth. Eine Untersuchung zu den Korintherbriefen* (FRLANT, N.F. 48) (Göttingen, 1956), p. 86.

[3] Pokorný, 'Epheserbrief und gnostische Mysterien', pp. 183 f.

[4] Where it is said of Anthropos that he διὰ τῆς ἁρμονίας παρέκυψεν, ἀναρρήξας τὸ κύτος.

occurs also in the similar context in *Corp. Herm.* iv. 6', he has touched on a very close parallel, since 'things mortal and things divine' are here called not only ἀμφότερα but also δύο... τῶν ὄντων. It is hardly correct, however, that *Corp. Herm.* i. 24–6 refers to the 'annihilation' of the wall blocking the way to heaven (the discussion is rather of passing through the various spheres); nor is it likely that the concept of peace in Ephesians is related to the discussion of the union of the masculine and feminine natures in man that is the subject of *Corp. Herm.* i. 15–21. Pokorný may be considered to have given additional strength to Schlier's first theory regarding the Anthropos, but to have come no closer to solving the problem at hand, nor to have demonstrated the place he ascribes to pre-Christian Judaism in the development from an earlier myth to Ephesians.

HEBREWS i. 3

Probably the most significant work to deal with the historical religious setting of Hebrews is that of Ernst Käsemann, *Das wandernde Gottesvolk*.[1] A major section of this work is entitled 'The Son and the Sons',[2] and it is the first part of this section, 'The Representation of the Son in Hebrews', that deals with the problem at hand.

Käsemann here sees Heb. i as presenting 'a firm Christological scheme..., in which the revelation of the Son attracts wider and wider circles and comprises various acts'.[3] This concept, he suggests, is similar to that in Phil. ii. 6–11, since in Heb. i. 3 f. 'the name "Son" appears...as the content of a κληρονομεῖν'. Here, as in Phil. ii. 7 f., 'Jesus' human history creates...the presuppositions for the official and heavenly proclamation of the Son'.[4] But this 'Son' is not for Käsemann the orthodox Christian Son of God, but rather 'Anthropos in the sense of the gnostic myth'.[5] Although the term χαρακτήρ may lead one to think of the 'rabbinic εἰκών concept...there can be no doubt concerning the Hellenistic coloring...of i. 3'.[6]

---

[1] Käsemann, *Das wandernde Gottesvolk* (FRLANT, N.F. 37) (Göttingen, 1961; first published 1938).   [2] *Ibid.* pp. 58–116.

[3] *Ibid.* pp. 60 f.   [4] *Ibid.* pp. 59 f.   [5] *Ibid.* p. 61.

[6] *Ibid.* p. 62. The role of the word ἀπαύγασμα, and the consequent relation between this hymn and the other New Testament Christological

Käsemann thinks that φέρειν is here also used in the technical sense 'of the Hellenistic aeon theology'.[1] As in the Philippians hymn, where the redeemer is related to the godhead by the synonymous μορφή, the redeemer of the present passage is seen to be the heavenly εἰκών, and 'Heb. i. 3, together with Col. i. 15 ff. and Phil. ii. 5 ff., evidently carries farther the same historical religious scheme that encounters us in the Hellenistic εἰκών doctrine and in the Sophia myth linked to it by this concept'.[2]

Heb. i. 3 and Phil. ii. 6–11 may be even more closely related: 'Philippians and Hebrews are distinguished only in that the effects of the obedience of Christ are cosmically related in the first instance, but are related to the community in the other instance. This obedience is then in the latter case understood cultically as "purification from sin".'[3]

Thus Käsemann has rightly seen the close relationship between the concepts of this hymn and those of the others that have been discussed. His discussion, however, significant as it is for an understanding of Hebrews, brings us no nearer a solution to the present problem.

C. Spicq makes the relation of the concepts employed in this hymn to pre-Christian Jewish Logos speculation obvious by the parallels he cites with Philo.[4] The Logos is called χαρακτήρ in *de Plantatione* 18, 'plays a role' in the 'creative activity' in *de Cherub.* 127, inherits creation (cf. Heb. i. 2) in *de Vita Mosis* i. 155; and, 'Both one and the other, like God himself,...quite exactly "bear it";...Philo, *Quis rerum divinarum heres sit* 36, ὁ τὰ μὴ ὄντα φέρων καὶ τὰ πάντα γεννῶν.'[5] It is, however, an inexact conclusion when Spicq refers to 'a probable influence... from the literary point of view'; for, as he himself notes,[6] the

hymns, is further clarified by F.-W. Eltester, p. 150, who notes, 'Philo can designate the spirit or the soul of man not only as ἀπαύγασμα (*de Opificio* 146) but also as χαρακτήρ (*Leg. Alleg.* iii. 95) and as εἰκών (*de Spec. Leg.* iii. 207) of the Logos'. Cf. further Sap. Sal. vii. 26, ἀπαύγασμα γάρ ἐστιν [*sc.* ἡ σοφία] φωτὸς ἀιδίου...καὶ εἰκὼν τῆς ἀγαθότητος αὐτοῦ [*sc.* τοῦ θεοῦ].

[1] Käsemann, *Das wandernde Gottesvolk*, p. 63.
[2] *Ibid.* p. 64.
[3] *Ibid.* p. 65.
[4] C. Spicq, *L'Épître aux Hébreux, I, Introduction* (Études Bibliques) (Paris, 1952); cf. also *II, Commentaire* (1953), *ad loc.*
[5] *Ibid.* pp. 49 f.   [6] *Ibid.* p. 70.

soteriological function ascribed to the redeemer in Heb. i. 3 is lacking in Philo. That the type of thinking exemplified by Philo is very closely related to the historical religious background of these Christological hymns is obvious; but Philo, Wisdom literature, and even the motif of the Suffering Righteous One in apocalyptic literature remain an incomplete solution to the historical religious problem.

I TIMOTHY iii. 16

Martin Dibelius also associated 'the exaltation into the sphere of the πνεῦμα' of this passage with Phil. ii. 9–11, i.e. with that part of the Philippians hymn dealing with the concept of exaltation. As proof of the assumption that ἐδικαιώθη refers to the exaltation, Dibelius offered Ode Sol. xxxi. 5: 'He himself was *accounted as righteous* [italics mine], for thus had his holy father promised him.' He also mentioned, however, the 'greeting to Horus at his introduction into the heavenly hall' as representing a similar concept of presentation connected with exaltation. Thus he suggested that the concept of the exaltation expressed in I Tim. iii. 16 may be only the general concept of the relatedness between exaltation and presentation before a higher deity.[1]

It is this view that is espoused by Joachim Jeremias,[2] who conceives the entire passage as a hymn of ascent to the throne and thus comes to a uniform interpretation based on the pattern Exaltation–Presentation–Enthronement before both the earthly and the heavenly world (in a chiastic pattern). It would seem, however, that a comparison of the first two lines of this passage with I Pet. iii. 18 (θανατωθεὶς μὲν σαρκί, ζωοποιηθεὶς δὲ πνεύματι) shows that the death, or at least the earthly existence, of Christ is referred to by the words ἐφανερώθη ἐν σαρκί. Some doubt, at least, is cast on the suggestion that this passage presents merely a universal concept of exaltation and presentation by the realization that the line ὤφθη ἀγγέλοις may refer to

[1] Dibelius, *Die Pastoralbriefe*, pp. 50 f. Cf. Virgil *Ecloga* iv. 15 f.: divisque videbit / permixtos heroas, et ipse videbitur illis; Eph. ii. 6 f.; iii. 9 ff.; Schweizer, *Erniedrigung und Erhöhung*, p. 105 n. 422.

[2] Jeremias, *Die Briefe an Timotheus und Titus* (NTD, 9) (Göttingen, 1947), p. 21.

the submission of the angels to the redeemer. Thus I Pet. iii. 19 seems to place the 'spirits in prison' at the same point in the drama at which I Tim. iii. 16 places the 'angels'.

I PETER iii. 18–22

In keeping with his views on Phil. ii. 6–11, Schweizer sees I Pet. iii. 18 as referring to the Righteous Suffering One. 'His righteousness is...evidenced here in his suffering, and precisely in his innocent suffering.'[1] Schweizer also sees this passage as being related to I Tim. iii. 16 in the formula, 'put to death in the flesh, made alive in the spirit'. Exaltation is 'in any case... the goal of the confession'.[2] On the basis of this comparison Schweizer thus suggests that ἐδικαιώθη in I Tim. iii. 16 is to be understood in the sense of νικᾶν, as in Rom. iii. 4 (= Ps. li. 6), and thus 'originally native only to Jewish thought'.[3]

The most thoroughgoing theological interpretation of I Pet. iii. 18 and its context has been the dissertation of Bo Reicke, *The Disobedient Spirits and Christian Baptism*.[4] Discussing the conjecture sometimes made that ἐν ᾧ, I Pet. iii. 19, represents an original 'Ενωχ, Reicke insists that this conjecture must be rejected, although he does see the passage as referring to the fallen angels of I Enoch. Going to the 'spirits' 'may be best understood as a duplicate or a typological correspondent to' the Enoch story.[5] Enoch, however, also fills the role of the Son of man in I Enoch; and 'we ought also to think of Enoch's character as "Primal Man" and the usual combination of this figure in primitive times with a corresponding figure in the last days, such as are shown by speculations as to the First and the Second Adam'.[6]

Reicke thinks that 'on the basis of the *Ode of Solomon* no. 24, it seems possible to assume that the Messianic scheme [in Judaism independent of Christianity] can really have involved

[1] Schweizer, *Erniedrigung und Erhöhung*, p. 55.
[2] *Ibid.* p. 108.   [3] *Ibid.* p. 105 n. 422.
[4] Bo Reicke, *The Disobedient Spirits and Christian Baptism. A Study of I Peter 3:19 and its Context* (Acta seminarii neotestamentici upsaliensis, 13) (Copenhagen, 1946).
[5] *Ibid.* pp. 100 f. Selwyn also, pp. 323, 329 f., sees parallels, but no more than that, with Enoch.
[6] Reicke, p. 102. Cf. further Scroggs, pp. 55 f.

a point where the saviour at the Descent comes into contact with the transgressors from the days of the Flood, without any special written passage originating such a theory'.[1] He renders this ode (in part) thus:

The Dove flew over the head of our Lord the Messiah...(3) And the inhabitants were afraid, and the sojourners were frightened. (4) The birds lifted their wings and fled, and the creepers died in their holes. (5) And the abysses were opened and closed, and they were seeking for the Lord, like (women) who are in travail. (6) But He was not given to them for food, because he did not belong to them. (7) And the abysses were indeed sealed by the seal of the Lord. And they perished in this thought, those who were from the beginning.[2] (8) For they became corrupt in the beginning, but the end of their corruption was life. (9) And every one of them that was defective perished, because it was not permitted to them to make a defence for themselves that they might remain.

SUMMARY

This examination of recent literature dealing with the problem of the historical religious background of the several New Testament Christological hymns, which has also served to call attention to the significant related texts, has shown that the background is in all probability to be sought in pre-Christian Judaism. Here there existed an emerging mythical configuration which could be attached, in the literature and in the religious consciousness of the Jew of the day, to various and different redeemer or revealer figures, above all Wisdom, Word, and Man (Adam). The possibility for this situation was given by the tendency to hypostatize divine qualities, but this tendency was no doubt then abetted by the movement toward a more highly developed myth, so that the tendency toward hypostatization and the tendency toward a mythical account of the activity of divine beings were united as one process.

[1] Reicke, p. 243.
[2] Reicke's translation of xxiv. 7 *b*, ܘܟ̇ܪܙܘ ܩܕܘ̈ ܡܣܝ̈ܒܪܝܢ ܗܘܘ ܠܗ ܘܠܐ ܐܬܝܗܒ, seems to be appropriate, and is supported by that of Bauer, *Die Oden Salomos*, 'und es gingen zugrunde an jenem Plan, die vormals gewesen waren'.

Within this emerging mythical configuration, it was possible to say of the divine figure that it was in the image (likeness, form) of God, i.e. that it possessed equality with God, that it participated in creation and embodied the All, that it descended from the sphere of the divine to the sphere of the mortal, that it in some way entered into human existence, i.e. became identified with human existence for the sake of the revelatory task. Although the figure of the Suffering Righteous One, which had acquired some of the characteristics of the divine figures, could be said to receive an exaltation, this remains in the area of vindication and seems therefore to form only a minor part of the mythical configuration that lies behind the New Testament Christological hymns. This role is perhaps present in Phil. ii. 6–11, where this figure may be seen possibly to have influenced the language, although hardly the conceptuality, of the hymn; and probably also in I Tim. iii. 16, where the exaltation is described as being 'vindicated in the spirit'—again more a merely linguistic similarity to the Servant than a material one, as neither I Tim. iii. 16 nor its context portrays the redeemer as in need of vindication. Since the originally foreign concept of a cosmic dualism can be seen in the Dead Sea Scrolls to have influenced some segments of pre-Christian Judaism, one is justified in assuming that such a dualism also found its way into those circles of Judaism where the process of hypostatization and the emerging mythical configuration indicated were to be found.[1]

From such a matrix, then, probably came the concepts found in the prologue of John (prior to i. 14) and in the first part of the other New Testament Christological hymns, with the exception of Eph. ii. 14–16. The historical religious background of the latter portion of the myth, however—that of the redeemer's effecting a cosmic reconciliation and of an exaltation and enthronement—is more problematical. The closest parallels to this myth are to be found in the later gnostic literature of the Mandaeans, of the Manichaeans, and of the *Corpus Hermeticum*. The New Testament Christological hymns can hardly be considered to have provided this concept to those gnostic groups, since it would in that case have to be argued that the gnostic

---

[1] Cf. Arthur Darby Nock, Review of *Gnosis und spätantiker Geist, Teil I* (1934), by Hans Jonas, *Gnomon*, vol. xii (1936), pp. 606–8.

97

groups bisected the myth as they found it, taking only the concept of a cosmic reconciliation but leaving the (to us) clearly Jewish portions of the myth.[1] Whence, then, came the myth present in these hymns into Christianity? Does the cosmic dualism present in the Dead Sea Scrolls mean that the myth of a primal Man–Redeemer elsewhere associated with that dualism was available to primitive Christianity, so that it could attach this myth to that of the Jewish divine figures? If this be true, it would of course mean that the Christ event became the magnet which drew these two concepts together. Or had the myth of a cosmic reconciliation already become a part of the developing myth in Judaism prior to Christianity, so that it provided a ready made explanation for the Christ event? It is the answer to this question that will engage us now.

[1] It would then also have to be argued that Christianity invented the myth of a cosmic reconciliation and attached it to the mythical configuration provided by its Jewish milieu. Although that is possible, other possibilities should also be suggested and investigated.

PART 3

HISTORICAL RELIGIOUS BACKGROUND OF THE NEW TESTAMENT CHRISTOLOGICAL HYMNS

CHAPTER 6

THE ODES OF SOLOMON

Throughout our review of the literature dealing with the New Testament Christological hymns, it was often suggested that the Odes of Solomon contained the closest parallels in any literature to the concept of the redeemer in the New Testament hymns. Thus the 'pure virgin' of Ode xxxiii seems to be identical with Sophia, yet is associated with the Word of revelation;[1] and creation in the Odes, as well as in the New Testament hymns, is thought of not as an original dualism, but in the Jewish sense—that is, that everything was created by God;[2] creation is thus not a tragedy in this literature.[3] The Odes of Solomon also show a stage in the hypostatization of the Word similar to, but less developed than, that of the prologue of John;[4] and it is further possible that Ode xxiv refers to a descent of the redeemer at which time he preached to the primordial transgressors.[5]

To this brief list derived from the discussion in Part 2 may be added several other significant parallels. The redeemer of the Odes of Solomon, who is not given a proper name other than Lord, is pre-existent with God and is the creator:

All was known to thee as God;
and set in order from the beginning before thee.

And thou, O Lord, hast made all things (iv. 14 f.).

He becomes himself man in order to fulfill his task as redeemer:

He became like me that I might receive him;
in similitude was he reckoned like me, that I might put him on.

And I trembled not when I saw him,
because (he is my grace).

Like my nature he became, that I might learn him,
and like my form, that I might not turn back from him (vii. 4–6).

---

[1] Above, p. 35.   [2] Above, p. 39.   [3] Above, p. 39.
[4] Odes xii, viii, and xlii; above, pp. 38 f.   [5] Above, pp. 95 f.

There is also a humiliation and exaltation:

> The man who was humbled,
>> and was exalted (for the sake of) his own righteousness
>> (xli. 12).

And the odist says,

> I gave praise to the Most High,
>> because he exalted his servant and the son of his handmaid
>> (xxix. 11).

Instead of the 'Name' being given to the redeemer, he gives his name to the redeemed ones (xlii. 20); yet it may be that this is only because he has first received the name; for the redeemer of the Odes of Solomon is clearly also the redeemed as well. Just prior to the 'naming' of xlii. 20, in fact, the Ode has offered this supplication: 'Let us also be saved with thee' (v. 18). The praise the redeemer receives can further be related to his name:

> (His praise he gave us for his name) (vi. 7).[1]

To the Lord of the Odes of Solomon there is not ascribed an *Allmachtsformel*, but the concept that the All was created by or proceeded from him seems to be involved when it is said,

> Everything is of the Lord.

> For thus (it) was from the beginning,
>> and to the end (vi. 3 f.).[2]

He is probably considered the reconciler of the All when he is said to be

> He who gathers the things that are betwixt (xxii. 2).

The Odes may be further linked to the Johannine hymn by the concepts Word, Light, Life, and Truth.[3] This is particularly obvious in Ode xli:

---

[1] This 'praising' or 'blessing' of the name is a prominent feature of the Odes of Solomon. Cf. Ode Sol. vi. 7; xvi. 20; (xviii. 1); xviii. 16; xx. 10; xxxi. 3; xxxix. 13; (xli. 5).

[2] One may object that this reference to the Lord is to God and not to a (secondary) redeemer. Yet there is a confusion in the Odes precisely at this point because of variant uses of the term 'Lord'; cf. below.

[3] Cf. Robert M. Grant, 'The Origin of the Fourth Gospel', *JBL*, vol. LXIX (1950), p. 321: The 'spiritual environment' of the author of the

The Father of *Truth* remembered me,
  he who (prepared) me from the beginning

  . . . .

And his *Word* is with us in all our way,
  the savior who makes *alive* and does not reject our souls.

  . . . .

The son of the Most High appeared
  in the perfection of his father;

And *light* dawned from the *Word*
  that was beforetime in him (xli. 9–14).

Also, Ode x. 1 f.:

The Lord hath directed my mouth by his *Word*,
  and he hath opened my heart by his *Light*.

And he hath caused to dwell in me his deathless *Life*.

With the light that shines into darkness, John i. 5, is to be
compared Ode xv. 1 f.:

As the sun is the joy to them that seek for its daybreak
  so is my joy the Lord.

Because he is my sun,
  and his rays have lifted me up,
  and his *light* hath dispelled all *darkness* from my face.

Parallel to John i. 11 f., 'His own received him not, but to as
many as received him, he gave power to become sons of God,
to those who believed in his name', is Ode xlii. 3 f.:

I became of no use
  to those who knew me,
  for I (should) hide myself from those
  who did not take hold of me;

But I will be with those
  who love me.

These parallels with the New Testament Christological hymns
are so close as to imply either influence from one to the other or

Gospel of John 'is that reflected in the Odes of Solomon and the epistles of
Ignatius'; also Bultmann (above, p. 37).

influence from a common background. Thus one must ask, Did these elements come into the Odes of Solomon from Christianity, or from somewhere else?

THE ODES OF SOLOMON AND CHRISTIANITY

The Christianity (or lack of it) of the Odes is at present still an open question. Almost as soon as the Odes had been discovered, Adolf Harnack pronounced them to be heterodox Jewish with Christian additions.[1] He saw Odes iv and vi as being definitely Jewish, and xix and xxvii as being purely Christian. Of all the rest, he held it to be either indifferent or problematical whether they were Jewish or Christian,[2] but he thought he could discern Christian elements in one-eighth of the total corpus.[3] Harnack's selection of Jewish and Christian elements in the Odes was arbitrary and evidently made quite hastily. Thus he made the mistake of thinking that every occurrence of the term 'Lord' was a Christian addition designating Christ. This it is not, since the term 'Lord' in the Odes is actually used most often with reference to God; for example, Ode iii. 6 refers to the Lord Most High, and when Ode iv refers to God in the first line and the Lord in the last line, these seem to be one and the same. Certainly Ode v. 1 f. makes the identification certain when it says:

> I (thank thee), O Lord,
>   because I love thee.

> O Most High, do not thou forsake me,
>   for thou art my hope.[4]

Gunkel challenged Harnack the following year,[5] showing for

---

[1] Adolf Harnack, *Ein jüdisch-christliches Psalmbuch aus dem ersten Jahrhundert* (Texte und Untersuchungen, 35, 4) (Leipzig, 1910).

[2] *Ibid.* p. 78.   [3] *Ibid.* p. 97.

[4] Harnack, had he realized this, could have used it to his advantage, for the use of the term Lord (Syr. ܡܳܪܝܳܐ, Heb. אדוני) to designate God reflects Jewish practice.

[5] Gunkel, 'Die Oden Salomos', *ZNW*, vol. XI (1910), pp. 291–328. The *ZNW* of that year contained two other articles dealing with the Odes of Solomon. One was by F. Schulthess, 'Textkritische Bemerkungen zu den syrischen Oden Salomos', *ibid.* pp. 249–57, and the other was by Friedrich Spitta, 'Zum Verständnis der Oden Salomos', *ibid.* pp. 193–203, 259–90.

the first time that the Odes were composed in *parallelismus membrorum*, and that this parallelism cut across the distinctions Harnack had attempted to make between Jewish and Christian elements in the Odes. In Ode iv there was 'nothing that a Christian could not also have said',[1] and the same was true for Ode vi. Gunkel maintained these same views later in his *RGG* article on the Odes.

Ode vii describes the incarnation of God; xix. 6 ff. relates the virgin birth; xix. 2 ff. and xxiii. 22 speak of the Father, Son, and Spirit. Also, viii. 10 ff.; x; xvii. 8*c* ff.; xxii; xxviii; and xlii are compositions on the person of Christ and sing, among other things, his suffering on the cross and his descent into hell; cf. xxxi; xli. 12 ff. Ode vi describes the triumph of Christianity, Ode xxiv the descent of the Spirit upon Christ.[2]

Gunkel admitted, however, that Christian concepts are often not *expressly* stated. He explained, 'Echoes of New Testament sayings are often heard, without being expressly quoted; most closely related are John and Paul'.

That the Odes contain Christian elements is not to be doubted, yet some of these are surely secondary. At least the Trinitarian formula of xxiii. 22 should be seen as a later Christianizing addition when it is realized that *v.* 21 had said that the letter alluded to was written 'wholly...by the finger of God'; whereas *v.* 22 seems to imply that Father, Son, and Holy Spirit were the joint authors. Also, in spite of the fact that there seem to be obvious references to the Cross and to the Virgin Birth,

Spitta, in his article, accepted Harnack's view that the Odes were partly Jewish, partly Christian, although he disagreed considerably over which parts were Christian. Cf. particularly Spitta, pp. 289 f. (the same general view was held by Gustav Diettrich, *Die Oden Salomos unter Berücksichtigung der überlieferten Stichengliederung* (Neue Studien zur Geschichte der Theologie und der Kirche, 9) (Berlin, 1911), and Hub. Grimme, *Die Oden Salomos syrisch-hebräisch-deutsch* (Heidelberg, 1911)). This formal division between Jewish and Christian elements was too complex to maintain, however, and when Gunkel wrote his *RGG* article on the Odes ('Salomo-Oden', *RGG*, edd. Gunkel and Leopold Tzscharnack, vol. v (1931[2]), cols. 87–90), he could say, 'Opposition has increasingly come forward against such separations (the last, G. Kittel, 'Oden Salomos, überarbeitet oder einheitlich?' 1914), so that these hypotheses can now be considered closed' ('Salomo-Oden', cols. 87 f.).

[1] Gunkel, 'Die Oden Salomos', p. 297.
[2] Gunkel, 'Salomo-Oden', col. 88.

there are central Christian elements missing from the Odes. Thus for example the words Jesus, Church, and Apostle do not occur. This indefinite state with regard to the Christianity of the Odes of Solomon evidently led Bultmann to think of them as having arisen outside of Christianity, for he consistently put the Odes together with the Mandaean literature as historical religious material for the study of the Gospel of John.[1] Harnack, in fact, seems to have been heading basically in the right direction in seeing both Jewish and Christian elements in the Odes, although his conclusions were incorrect. If the formal unity of the Odes is now generally granted,[2] it would still seem to be a mistake, in view of the preliminary observations just made, to explain the concepts found in the Odes of Solomon as having arisen originally within Christianity. Thus we must raise the question of the origin of some of the relevant concepts contained in the Odes.

THE LORD OF THE ODES OF SOLOMON

Certainly it should be realized that the Odes of Solomon give evidence of a thoroughgoing *eclecticism* in their religious ideas. Gunkel, after he had shown Harnack to be wrong in making formal distinctions in the Odes between Jewish and Christian elements, showed the true mettle of his scholarship by interpreting them to be the creation of a community which he described as 'men of Jewish origin strongly influenced by Christianity'. He also saw in the Odes elements from oriental mythology, Greek philosophy, and 'mystery-wisdom'.[3]

This religious eclecticism involved in the Odes of Solomon is to be observed, in addition to other places, in the use of the term 'Lord' to designate both God and redeemer, and in the relation of the term ‏ܡܫܝܚܐ‎, 'Anointed, Messiah', to the term 'Lord'.[4] The word ‏ܡܫܝܚܐ‎ occurs seven times in the Odes. Three of

[1] This position is now also taken by Kurt Rudolph. Cf. particularly 'War der Verfasser der Oden Salomos ein "Qumran-Christ"?', *Revue de Qumran*, vol. IV (1963–4), pp. 528–35.

[2] Cf. Gunkel, 'Salomo-Oden', cols. 87 f.

[3] *Ibid.* col. 89.

[4] Both Harnack and Gunkel supposed that the application of the term Messiah to the redeemer was a Christian element. So also Spitta, Diettrich, and Grimme. This has become a proof of undetermined significance to later

these times (ix. 3; xxix. 6; and xli. 3) it is the Old Testament term 'the Lord's Anointed'.[1] An occurrence in xli. 15 should probably also fall into the same category, since xli. 3 uses the term in this way, but this is not certain. In the remaining three occurrences, xvii. 16; xxiv. 1; and xxxix. 11, the two terms 'Lord' and 'Messiah' are used absolutely together, ܡܫܝܚܐ ܡܪܝܐ (ܡܪܝ) ܡܪܝܐ. A comparable situation is to be observed in one place in the Psalms of Solomon, where one reads in Ps. Sol. xvii. 32, βασιλεὺς αὐτῶν χριστὸς κυρίου, while the Syriac reads (Syriac *v.* 36) ܡܠܟܗܘܢ ܡܫܝܚܐ ܡܪܝܐ 'their king is the Messiah, the Lord'. One might think, because of this change between the Greek and Syriac of Ps. Sol. xvii. 32 (36), that the three occurrences of the term 'Lord Messiah' in the Odes of Solomon are not original, but were brought about by the deliberate omission of a ܝ to produce the Christian reading ܡܫܝܚܐ ܡܪܝܐ, χριστὸς κύριος. Since this is, however, the reverse of the term as it occurs in the Odes, it seems more likely that the use of both terms should be ascribed to the writer(s) of the Odes of Solomon, and that such usage reflects the confusion in the Odes regarding the recipient of the designation 'Lord', who can be both God and redeemer (Messiah).

The problem of the dual significance of the term 'Lord' is posed most pointedly by Ode xvii:

1 I was crowned by my God,
   and my crown is living;

2 And I was justified by my Lord,
   and my salvation is incorruptible.

3 I was loosed from vanities,
   and I am not condemned.

4 The (bonds) were cut off by (her) [*sic*][2] hands;
   I received the face and the fashion of a new person,
   and I walked in him [*sc.* the new person] and was redeemed.

5 And the thought of Truth led me,
   and I walked after it and did not wander.

scholarship, however, as is seen in the fact that Walter Bauer, *Die Oden Salomos*, regularly translates ܡܫܝܚܐ simply as 'der Gesalbte'.

[1] Cf. e.g. Ps. ii. 2; xviii. 51; xxviii. 8; lxxxiv. 10.
[2] Refers evidently to the crown, which is Truth; cf. *v.* 5; ix. 8.

6 And all (who saw) me were amazed,
   and I was supposed by them to be a strange person.

7 And he who knew and brought me up is the Most High in
   all his perfection;
   and he glorified me by his Kindness,
   and raised my thought to the height of Truth.

8 And from thence he gave me the way of his steps,
   and I opened the doors that were closed;

9 And I broke in pieces the bars of iron;
   (my own iron) melted and dissolved before me;

10 And nothing appeared closed to me,
   because I was the opening of everything.

11 And I went towards all (of mine, who were bound), to
   loose them,
   that I might not leave any man bound and binding;

12 And I imparted my knowledge without grudging,
   and (my request) with my love.

13 And I sowed my fruits in hearts,
   and transformed them through myself;

14 And they received my blessing and lived,
   and they were gathered to me and were saved,

15 Because they became to me as my own members,
   and I was their head.

16 Glory to thee our Head, Lord, Messiah.

Hallelujah.

Here the *parallelismus membrorum* in *vv.* 1 and 2 shows that God
is first called 'Lord', but the praise of *v.* 16 is given to the Lord
Messiah, the redeemer; thus, there seems to be a 'shift' somewhere in the Ode, whereby the 'Lord' in the second sense
becomes the speaker.[1] Harris indicated this 'shift' by the
insertion of 'Christ speaks' before *v.* 6. But is there really such

[1] R. Abramowski, 'Der Christus der Salomooden', *ZNW*, vol. xxxv
(1936), pp. 44–69, explains these phenomena by taking recourse to the
concept of two sons, and supposes that the blurring of the distinctions between singer, redeemer, and God is the result of a confusion of the earthly
with the heavenly son. Cf. particularly *ibid.* p. 67.

a change? Does one not in fact see in Ode xvii the raising of the odist to the position of the redeemer, in which position he can also be called Lord along with God, who is addressed as Lord in *v.* 2?

The confusion or alternation in the use of the term 'Lord' in the Odes of Solomon is too hastily explained by the suggestion of the coming of Christianity to a Jewish community. This phenomenon might be explained equally well—or even more adequately—as the result of influence on a Jewish group from some other religion, specifically that of Adonis.[1] Here there is a redeemer figure who goes by no other name than that of Lord, Ἄδωνις (אדון). Could a Jewish group have been influenced by the worship of Adonis to the extent that it came to use the common term Adonai (Syriac ܡܪܝܐ) in both ways, i.e. in the Jewish sense and also in the sense of the worshippers of Adonis? A precedent for such a situation is certainly given by the cult of Sabazius in Asia Minor. Here some Jews identified the cultic redeemer *Sabazius* with Yahweh *Sabaoth* and considered him to be a redeemer figure secondary to the high god, Θεὸς Ὕψιστος.[2] Adonis, it should be remembered, is the western designation of Tammuz[3] (or, viewed otherwise, Tammuz is regularly designated simply 'the Lord'),[4] and his influence was felt on Jewish religion before the time of Ezekiel,[5] as is attested by Ezek. viii.

---

[1] The fact that there is a considerable confusion in the Odes regarding the *redeemer* seems to show that the concept of a redeemer has been superimposed upon the older body of ideas. The points of contact between these two traditions may have lain in the term 'Lord'.

[2] Cf. Franz Cumont, 'Les Mystères de Sabazius et le Judaïsme', *Comptes Rendus de l'Académie des inscriptions et belles-lettres* (1906), pp. 63–79, particularly pp. 64 f. This Jewish Sabazius was accorded, at least in Bithynia, the title πανκοίρανος, i.e. παντοκράτωρ (*ibid.* pp. 68 f.). Cf. further Colin Roberts, Theodore C. Skeat, and Arthur Darby Nock, 'The Gild of Zeus Hypsistos', *Harvard Theological Review*, vol. XXIX (1936), p. 63.

[3] Wolf Wilhelm Baudissin, *Adonis und Esmun* (Leipzig, 1911), p. 81; Karl Preisendanz, 'Tammuz', *Paulys Real-Encyclopädie der classischen Altertumswissenschaft*, edd. Wilhelm Kroll and Karl Mittelhaus (Neue Bearbeitung begonnen von Georg Wissowa, 1932), 2. Reihe, vol. IV, 2, col. 2140.

[4] Heinrich Zimmern, 'Der babylonische Gott Tamūz', *Abhandlungen der königlich-sächsischen Gesellschaft der Wissenschaften*, philolog.-hist. Klasse, 27 (1909), p. 8. Zimmern suggests, 'Perhaps the prototype to Adonis is present in this designation, insofar as this name must go back to Canaanite אדן Adon "Lord".'

[5] Zimmern, *ibid.* p. 4, notes but does not discuss the parallelism between Tammuz and 'many traits' of Jewish Messiah concepts.

14: 'Then he brought me to the entrance of the north gate of the house of the Lord; and behold, there sat women weeping for Tammuz.'

Tammuz (Adonis) elements are almost surely to be recognized in the Odes of Solomon.[1] Thus when the redeemer gives his milk to his chosen ones (Ode viii. 16) one is reminded of Tammuz' role as shepherd, and 'of the milk, which the shepherd gives with his pure hands';[2] Tammuz is also called *Ama-ga* (= Mother + Milk).[3] When the milk is called the 'dew of the Lord' (Ode Sol. xxxv. 5) this associates the concept still more strongly with Adonis/Tammuz who, as god of vegetation and of spring, brings rain and dew.[4] The reference to planting and trees in Ode Sol. xi. 18 f. may refer to the Adonis gardens;[5] and when Ode xxiv. 5 f. refers to those who 'were seeking for the Lord, like (women) in travail; and he was not given to them for food', this seems to be a clear allusion to the wailing of women for the departed *grain god* Adonis *after he was killed*, i.e. at the time of the summer festival:[6]

The hero, your lord,   has suffered destruction,
The god of grain, the child,   your lord, has suffered destruction.[7]

---

[1] In Assyrian, Tammuz (Sumerian *Dumu-zi*) was *māru kēnu* (*ibid.* p. 6; note the similarity of sound between the Assyrian word *māru* and the Syriac *marya'*). This name means 'true son'; does one then see a reflection of this in the term ‏ܡܪܝܐ‎ ‏ܒܪܐ‎, 'Son of Truth', or 'true son', in Ode xxiii. 18?

[2] Preisendanz, col. 2141.

[3] *Cuneiform Texts from Babylonian Tablets, &c., in the British Museum* (London, 1896–), vol. xxiv, 19, ll. c and d, with duplicate *CT*, vol. xxiv, 9; quoted in Zimmern, p. 7 n. 1.

[4] Baudissin, *Adonis und Esmun*, pp. 166–8.

[5] Cf. Stephen Langdon (ed.), *Sumerian and Babylonian Psalms* (Paris, 1909), pp. 300 f.; Baudissin, *Studien zur semitischen Religionsgeschichte*, vol. ii (Leipzig, 1878), p. 185. One may not exclude, however, the motif of planting in Judaism.

[6] Baudissin, *Adonis und Esmun*, p. 141: 'The lament for the dead Adonis is performed in midsummer.'

[7] Langdon, pp. 320 f. The way in which the odist becomes the divine redeemer in Ode xvii may also reflect Babylonian cultic usage. Thus in a hymn quoted by Zimmern in 'Babylonische Hymnen und Gebete in Auswahl', *Der alte Orient*, vol. vii, 3 (1905), p. 22, Ištar is addressed in the second person and then speaks herself in the first person. Regarding the regular change from second to first person in Babylonian hymns cf. Norden, *Agnostos Theos*, p. 207.

Lord, child of the great prince, mighty in heaven and in the
  underworld,
  we praise thy name as Great when thou, coming from on
    high, dost go down into the underworld amidst laments.[1]

Tammuz is called 'the Man of the lament';[2] and the wail is
heard in the words:

O, the King, the perfect Man, the Only One!
The Wild Bull, Tammuz, the perfect Man, the Only One!
O, the King is locked up in a dark place![3]

Adonis is associated with floods and rivers, as is regular for
Phoenician male deities,[4] and a river near Byblos was named
Adonis.[5] Thus may be explained the references in Ode vi.
8 ff.;[6] xxvi. 13; and xxx. 1 ff. to the river that flows from the
Lord bringing salvation. Particularly to be noted is Ode xxxix.
1–4:

Mighty rivers are the power of the Lord,
  which carry headlong
    those that despise him,

And entangle their paths,
  and sweep away their fords,

And carry off their bodies,
  and destroy their souls;

For they are more swift than lightning,
  and more rapid.

Finally, Ode Sol. xlii. 11 should be noted, which says, 'Sheol
saw me and was in distress; death cast me up and many along
with me'. This is also reminiscent of songs to Tammuz:

[1] *CT*, vol. xv, 8, ll. 1 f., quoted in P. Maurus Witzel, *Tammuz-Liturgien
und Verwandtes* (Analecta Orientalia, 10) (Rome, 1935), p. 5.

[2] *Ibid.* p. 78.

[3] *Ibid.* p. 105; cf. further James G. Frazer, *Adonis, Attis, Osiris* (London,
1906), pp. 132 f.

[4] Baudissin, *Adonis und Esmun*, p. 27.

[5] *Ibid.* pp. 72 f.

[6] Which does not refer, as Gunkel ('Die Oden Salomos', p. 297) showed,
to the Jewish figure of the stream of salvation which was to flow forth from
the Temple.

He goes, he flees away to the breast of the earth,

. . . .

On the path, which brings an end to people, which brings
men to rest,

. . . .

The manly one, to the far earth, which is invisible;[1]

and

On the day when Tammuz ascends (?),
  With him the flute of lapis lazuli, the ring of carnelian
  ascend (?),
With him mourners, men and women, ascend (?),
[Then] the dead shall ascend and offer incense.[2]

The confusion, then, in the Odes of Solomon between the use
of the term 'Lord' to designate the Most High and the use of
the same term to designate the redeemer may be explained by
the influence of the worship of Adonis on one segment of the
Jewish worship of Adonai. Although the presence of some
Christian elements (some of which may be viewed as secondary
additions) in the Odes of Solomon is certainly not denied, the
presence of elements related to the cult of Adonis must also be
recognized. These elements, together with the use of the word
'Lord' to refer to the redeemer—a usage which is inconsistent
with the other (Jewish) use of the word in the Odes to refer to
God—make it highly questionable that the distinctive view of
the redeemer presented in the Odes is to be explained as the
result of influence from the New Testament tradition.[3] The

---

[1] 'Leichenlied um Tammuz', in Hugo Gressmann, *Altorientalische Texte
und Bilder zum Alten Testament*, vol. 1: *Texte* (Berlin, 1926), p. 271.

[2] 'Die Höllenfahrt der Ištar', *ibid.* p. 210.

[3] Grant, 'The Odes of Solomon and the Church of Antioch', *JBL*,
vol. LXIII (1944), pp. 368 f.; Georg Beer, 'Salomo-Oden', *Paulys Real-
Encyclopädie der classischen Altertumswissenschaft*, 2. Reihe, vol. 1, 2, edd.
Wilhelm Kroll and Kurt Witte (Neue Bearbeitung begonnen von Georg
Wissowa, 1920), cols. 1999 f.; also 'Pseudepigraphen des AT.s, II, A: Die
Psalmen und Oden Salomos', *PRE*, vol. XXIV, ed. Albert Hauck (1913³),
p. 377; and Schulz, 'Salomo-Oden', *RGG*, vol. V, ed. Kurt Galling (1961³),
col. 1340, think of the Odes of Solomon as originating completely within
Christianity. Nearer the view espoused here is that of Walter Baumgartner,
'Das trennende Schwert Oden Salomos 28, 4', *Zum Alten Testament und
seiner Umwelt. Ausgewählte Aufsätze* (Leiden, 1959), p. 274. Rudolph, in 'War

eclecticism present in the Odes of Solomon prevents a final explanation of the character of the redeemer they present simply in terms of a fusion between concepts from Judaism and from the cult of Adonis; still, the Odes of Solomon seem to attest that Judaism could, under some outside influence, give birth to at least one myth of redemption similar to that displayed in the New Testament Christological hymns, and yet apparently independent of the New Testament tradition. If this could occur independently of the New Testament, then presumably also prior to it; therefore, the possibility is increased that the element of cosmic reconciliation, which completes the act of redemption, had already become a part of the developing myth lying behind the New Testament Christological hymns prior to its appropriation by Christianity. The redeemer of the Odes of Solomon certainly effects redemption by incorporating the redeemed, as is clear from Ode xvii. 14 f.:

They received my blessing and lived,
    and they were gathered to me and were saved,

Because they became to me as my own members,
    and I was their head.

That redemption has a cosmic aspect receives little attention from the odist, but such seems to be involved in Ode xxii. 2,

He who gathers the things that are betwixt.

The possibility that the myth in the New Testament Christological hymns was already intact prior to its use by Christianity is still further increased when it is seen that the redeemer myth of the Odes of Solomon is connected with a stage of hypostatization of divine qualities less developed than the stage present in the New Testament Christological hymns.

der Verfasser der Oden Salomos ein "Qumran-Christ"?', p. 527, is in the middle in ascribing the Odes to 'a Christianity of Syrian origin stamped by Gnosticism'. Rudolph seems not to have investigated the possibility of influence from the Adonis cult although he might logically have done so.

HYPOSTATIZATION IN THE ODES OF SOLOMON

Particularly noticeable is the Wisdom-like figure of Ode xxxiii. *Vv.* 1–4 seem to indicate that this figure's name is Goodness, ܛܒܘܬܐ,[1] but the obscurity of these verses leaves some doubt. At any rate, a perfect virgin (*v.* 5)[2] proclaims to the sons of man,

> I will enter into you
> and bring you forth from destruction,
> and I will make you wise in the ways of Truth.

> .   .   .   .

> Hear ye me and be saved,
> for the (Goodness) of God I am telling among you (*vv.* 8, 10).

Thus there is this one instance in which a divine figure, very similar to the hypostatized figures of Sophia and Logos, proclaims salvation through knowledge.[3]

One should perhaps name this lady in Ode xxxiii 'Truth', since she refers to 'the ways of Truth' and since Truth is elsewhere a hypostasis in the Odes of Solomon. Of the thirty-four occurrences of the word 'truth', ܩܘܫܬܐ, in the Odes of Solomon, one should note at least the following. In Ode Sol. viii. 8 the odist makes a call to

> Hear the Word of Truth,
> and receive the knowledge of the Most High.

What then follows is the words of the Most High, who tells how he 'fashioned mind and heart (according to my will)' (*v.* 20); but the parallelism between Truth and the Most High in *v.* 8 makes one wonder whether Truth is not also considered to be present at this fashioning in a way similar to Sophia in Sap. ix. 9, who 'was present when thou [*sc.* God] didst make the world'. The 'words of Truth' are mentioned again in xii. 1, and when Truth, 'like the flow of waters, flows...from my mouth' (xii.

---

[1] Ulrich Wilckens, *Weisheit und Torheit* (Beiträge zur historischen Theologie, 26) (Tübingen, 1959), p. 137: 'The "Goodness of God" is here herself presented as a person.'

[2] Cf. Philo *de Fuga et Inv.* 50, where Sophia is called a virgin.

[3] Cf., however, Reitzenstein, *Das iranische Erlösungsmysterium* (Bonn am Rhein, 1921), pp. 241 f., who likens Ode xxxiii to the 'teaching of the Christian Gnostic Justin'. Wilckens on the other hand, p. 135, considers this Ode a 'connecting link' between Jewish and gnostic Wisdom speculation; cf. also *ibid.* p. 138.

2), Truth is certainly thought of as somewhat substantial and as capable of acting somewhat independently. In Ode Sol. ix. 8 it is said of Truth:

> An everlasting crown is Truth;
>   blessed are they who set it on their heads,

which is to be compared with Ode Sol. i. 1: 'The Lord is upon my head like a crown'; and in Ode xiv. 7 Truth is the one who teaches the odist his songs. Also, Ode Sol. xxxii. 2 speaks of the Word which emanates from the Truth, or *originates from itself.* Thus both the hypostatization of Truth and its (her) interchangeability with other hypostases seem to be attested for the Odes of Solomon. Wisdom is perhaps present once as an hypostasis in the Odes: 'He who created Wisdom is wiser than his works' (vii. 8).[1]

More important for our present interest is the fact that the Word gains considerable prominence as an hypostasis in the Odes. This statement is not entirely accurate, for there are in reality two hypostatized Words, ﬈﬈﬈, *melta'*, which is feminine,[2] and ﬈﬈﬈, *petgama'*, which is masculine.[3] These two words occur almost an equal number of times in the following contexts:

Melta:

> x. 1 The Lord hath directed my mouth *b^emeltah*
>   and he hath opened my heart by his light.

> xii. 8 By him [*sc. petgama', v.* 3] the worlds spake to (one
>   another)
>   and those that were silent (became) *b^emelta'*.

> xv. 9 Sheol hath been abolished *b^emelti* [*sc.* of the odist].

---

[1] A number of 'hypostases in the making' (Ringgren) are also to be found in the Odes. Cf. e.g. ﬈﬈, Ode iv. 3; viii. 20; xvi. 19; xxviii. 19; xxx. 5; xli. 10; ﬈﬈﬈, Ode vi. 6; vii. 7, 13, 21; viii. 8; xi. 4; xv. 5; xxiii. 4; ﬈﬈﬈, Ode viii. 5, 21; ix. 10; xxv. 10. Reitzenstein, *Das iranische Erlösungsmysterium,* p. 91, pointed out that '*utara*', Ode xli. 10, and *maḥsabta*', xxiii. 5, appear to be parallel to early stages of Mandaean hypostatization. Reitzenstein thought of the Odes as being later than the Mandaean literature, however (*ibid.* p. 91). Regarding hypostatization in the Odes of Solomon, cf. also Schulz, 'Salomo-Oden', col. 1340.

[2] This seems to be the case here, although *melta'* becomes masculine in the Peshitta, where it translates λόγος.

[3] פִּתְגָם is the regular Aramaic equivalent in the Targums for דָּבָר; cf. Moore, p. 417.

xvi. 7   The strength of his *melta'* [*sc.* of the Lord]...

xvi. 8   The *melta'* of the Lord searches out the unseen thing.

xvi. 14   The hosts (obey) his [*sc.* the Lord's] *melta'*.

xvi. 19   The worlds were made *b*ᵉ*meltah* [*sc.* the Lord's] and by the thought of his heart.

xxix. 9   [The Lord authorized the odist] to make war *b*ᵉ*meltah*.

xxix. 10   The Lord overthrew my enemy *b*ᵉ*meltah*.

xxxix. 9   The Lord has bridged them [*sc.* the rivers] *b*ᵉ*meltah*.

xli. 11   His *melta'* [*sc.* of the Father of Truth, *v.* 9] is with us in all our way.

xli. 14   Light dawned from the *melta'*.

Petgama:

vii. 7   The Father of Knowledge
is the *petgama'* of Knowledge.

viii. 8   Hear the *petgama'* of Truth
and receive the Knowledge of the Most High.

ix. 3   The *petgama'* of the Lord and his good pleasures...

xii. 3   (He) [an indefinite reference, cf. *v.* 1; appears to refer to the Most High] has caused (his) knowledge to abound in me
because the mouth of the Lord is the *petgama'* (which is true).

xii. 5   The swiftness of the *petgama'* is inexpressible (?).

xii. 10   They [*sc.* the worlds, *v.* 8] were stimulated *man petgama'*,
and they knew him that made them.

xii. 12   The dwelling place of the *petgama'* is (the Son of) man, and his Truth is love.

xii. 13   Blessed are they who by (this) [*sc.* by the *petgama'*] have comprehended (ܐܣܬܟܠܘ) everything and who have known the Lord by his Truth.

xviii. 4   Do not (cast off from me) thy *petgama'*.

xxiv. 9   It was not permitted to them to make a defence
(*petgama'*) for themselves.

xxxii. 2   The *petgama'* from the Truth, (which [m., i.e. the
petgama'] stems from itself).

xxxvii. 3   His *petgama'* [*sc.* of the Most High, *v.* 1] came to
me.

xlii. 14   I spake with them with living lips
in order that my *petgama'* may not be void.

The genders of these two hypostases appear to be the clue for
understanding at least a part of the differences between them.
The Melta is usually an instrument of God's action (note the
frequency of the phrase *b^emeltah*), and thus falls into the line of
feminine hypostases in Judaism, headed by Wisdom, who are
pre-existent with God and who assist him at creation and in the
further carrying out of his will. One should note that in the one
place where Melta is used in the same context with Petgama
(xii. 8) the word does not have the sense of an hypostasis, but the
clause means 'those who were silent acquired speech'.

Regarding the masculine word for Word, Petgama,[1] however, a different situation exists. Whereas Melta is never
associated with Truth and Knowledge, Petgama regularly is,
and seems indeed to be equated with Truth.[2] Thus when the
Petgama emanates from Truth, it emanates from itself (xxxii. 2),
and such an identification is certainly in the background when
xii. 3 refers to the '*petgama'* (which is true)'. It is not clear what
vii. 7, which equates the Father with the Petgama, means, but
the equation is certainly made. The Melta is never a completely
independent being; but when the swiftness of the Petgama is
referred to (xii. 5), and when it is said that he 'came to me'
(xxxvii. 3), one sees that the Petgama can be fully independent.
The same seems also to be implied by xii. 10, where the worlds,
'stimulated (from) the *petgama'*...knew him that made them'.
Here 'stimulation' and 'making' mean the same thing.

[1] As with Melta, there is one occurrence of Petgama which clearly does
not denote an hypostasis, xxiv. 9, where it merely means that which one says
in one's defense.

[2] As a syzygy?

It would seem to be quite difficult to explain these separate hypostases as *outgrowths* of the Johannine Logos. Certainly no reason can be advanced why the Logos of John i would have been translated into two Words. Rather it would make more sense to suppose that both these traditions developed independently of the *Vorlage* of the prologue of John,[1] and that the Logos of John i represents a more advanced stage of hypostatization, or perhaps rather an independent tradition. The parallels between the Johannine prologue and the Odes of Solomon have of course been pointed out above, particularly with regard to Ode vii; it remains to indicate more clearly how the Logos of the Johannine hymn is related to the concept of Word in the Odes of Solomon, with regard both to the Melta and to the Petgama.

Ode xxxii. 2 refers to the autogenesis of the Petgama. This is not exactly the same as the concept expressed by the ἐν ἀρχῇ of John i. 1, but it does seem to refer to a primordial event. The equation of God and Word, however (John i. 1, θεὸς ἦν ὁ λόγος), is certainly made with regard to the Petgama in Ode vii. 7, where Father and Petgama are paralleled. πάντα δι᾿ αὐτοῦ ἐγένετο, John i. 3, can be related to both Petgama and Melta, as in Ode xii (*vv.* 8 and 10), where the Petgama is the agent of creation, and Ode xvi. 19, where the Melta is put in the same position. The relation of the Word to the Light in John i is an oblique relation, the Life which is in the Word being the true Light (John i. 4 f.). In the Odes of Solomon, the connection between Word and Light is more direct, but is nevertheless certainly to be compared with the Johannine concept. Thus in x. 1 the Melta is paralleled to the Light, and in xli. 14 it is said that 'Light dawned from the Melta'. Consequently, when in John i. 5 the light shines into darkness, this can be paralleled in

[1] It should be emphasized that it is immaterial that the Odes of Solomon were actually composed later than the composition of that *Vorlage*. The traditions may be older and the Odes later than John. It is the realization that the use of the words Petgama and Melta in the Odes of Solomon could hardly be explained as due to Johannine influence that renders ineffectual such conclusions as that of F.-M. Braun (L'énigme des Odes de Solomon', *Revue Thomiste*, vol. LVII (1957), p. 619) that, because the Fourth Gospel is earlier, the author of the Odes must have known the Gospel 'without a doubt firsthand'. The Odes are generally dated in the first half of the second century A.D.; cf. Schulz, 'Salomo-Oden', col. 1339.

the Odes by xvi. 8, 'The Melta...searches out the unseen thing'. That the darkness did not overcome the light, John i. 5, might thus be related to Ode xv. 9, where Sheol is abolished by the Melta. Consequently also, when John i. 9 refers to τὸ φῶς τὸ ἀληθινόν, this is formally comparable to Ode xii. 3, ܘܗ ܟܠܡ ; also related is Ode viii. 8, which refers to the Petgama of Truth. John i. 10 says of the Word (now referred to obliquely as the Light) that the world did *not* know him when he came into it. Over against this, Ode xii. 10 says that the worlds *did* know 'him that made them', i.e. the Petgama. It thus seems that there is present in the Johannine passage here an advance beyond the tradition in Ode Sol. xii, whereby the cosmic dualism also becomes more pronounced.

An analysis of features in the Odes of Solomon related to the New Testament Christological hymns has thus shown that the concept of the redeemer in the Odes need not be explained as a further development of the redeemer motif in the New Testament, and that it is in fact probably better to be explained as the result of influence from other religions, especially that of Adonis; further, that hypostatization in the Odes of Solomon, particularly the hypostatization of the Word, has proceeded independently of the prologue of John and is in some respects logically prior in its development to the hypostasis of the Logos in the prologue of John. A third point, which is obvious but has not been explicitly stated, is that the process of hypostatization of divine qualities has not come together into a unity in the Odes of Solomon with the figure of the cultic redeemer. In the New Testament Christological hymns, however, the element of cosmic reconciliation—which seems to have come from the ancient eastern concept of the reconstitution of the macro-Anthropos—has already become a part of the developing myth, has already been integrated into the mythical configuration associated primarily with the hypostases. If the redeemer concept and the stage of hypostatization evidenced in the Odes of Solomon are not to be explained as the result of influence from the New Testament, neither, however, would the reverse be correct. That would give too simple an answer, and would be historically unjustifiable. The relevance of the Odes of Solomon for understanding the historical religious background of the New Testament Christological hymns is rather that they reveal that motifs highly similar to those of the New Testament Christological hymns could, at a period not far from the first use of those hymns by Christianity, be utilized by one segment of Judaism. If, independently of the New Testament and almost contemporary with it, all the leading elements of the New Testament Christological hymns—hypostatization of divine qualities in a developing myth, redemption involving reunification of the disparate elements, cosmic reconciliation at least hinted at—could be present in one corpus of literature produced by a Jewish sect,[1] then the possibility becomes much greater that the combination of the elements present in the New Testament Christological hymns had occurred already in pre-Christian Judaism.

[1] It is readily admitted, and should in fact be emphasized, that this sect also apparently received some influence from emerging Christianity. That does not alter the above analysis, which has shown that the several motifs under consideration are less far along in their development in the Odes of Solomon than in the New Testament Christological hymns.

CHAPTER 7

THE COPTIC GNOSTIC LITERATURE
FROM NAG HAMMADI

THE GOSPEL OF TRUTH

One body of literature that has aroused particular interest among New Testament scholars in recent years is the Coptic gnostic literature discovered at Nag Hammadi in 1945.[1] These materials are just beginning to be assessed in any comprehensive way, primarily because the texts have been so long appearing, a situation which has caused scholars to have to work from translations or even reviews. The Coptic of a fair number of the writings is now available,[2] however, and it is one of these, the so-called Gospel of Truth (GT), that is now to be discussed.

To begin with, it should be noted that there are many close

[1] Regarding the finds, cf. W. C. van Unnik, *Evangelien aus dem Nilsand*, trans. Jean Landré (Frankfurt am Main, 1960), pp. 9 ff.

[2] *Evangelium Veritatis*, edd. Michel Malinine, H.-Ch. Puech, and Gilles Quispel (Zurich, 1956); pp. 33–6, missing from this *editio princeps*, have appeared as a supplement to the first-named work (1961); *The Gospel According to Thomas*, edd. A. Guillaumont, *et al.* (New York, 1959); *Coptic Gnostic Papyri in the Coptic Museum at Old Cairo*, ed. Pahor Labib (Cairo, 1956 ff.); Søren Giversen, *Apocryphon Johannis. The Coptic Text of the Apocryphon Johannis in the Nag Hammadi Codex II with Translation, Introduction and Commentary* (Acta Theologica Danica, 5) (Copenhagen, 1963); *Die drei Versionen des Apokryphon des Johannes im Koptischen Museum zu Alt-Kairo*, edd. Martin Krause and Pahor Labib, *Abhandlungen des Deutschen Archäologischen Instituts Cairo*, Koptische Reihe, 1 (Wiesbaden, 1962); *Die koptisch-gnostische Schrift ohne Titel aus Codex II von Nag Hammadi im Koptischen Museum zu Alt-Kairo*, edd. Alexander Böhlig and Pahor Labib (Deutsche Akademie der Wissenschaften zu Berlin, Institut für Orientforschung, 58) (Berlin, 1962); *De resurrectione (Epistula ad Rheginum)*, edd. Michel Malinine, *et al.* (Zurich, 1963); *Koptisch-gnostische Apokalypsen aus Codex V von Nag Hammadi im Koptischen Museum zu Alt-Kairo*, edd. Alexander Böhlig and Pahor Labib (= *Wissenschaftliche Zeitschrift der Martin-Luther-Universität*, Sonderband, 1963); cf. the related texts, *Die gnostischen Schriften des koptischen Papyrus Berolinensis 8502*, ed. Till (Texte und Untersuchungen zur Geschichte der altchristlichen Literatur, 60) (Berlin, 1955). Cf. further the comprehensive articles by James M. Robinson, 'The Coptic Gnostic Library Today', *NTS*, vol. XIV (1968), pp. 356–401; and Kurt Rudolph, 'Gnosis und Gnostizismus, ein Forschungsbericht', *ThR*, vol. XXXIV (1969), pp. 121–75, 181–231, 358–61.

similarities between passages in the Gospel of Truth and the New Testament Christological hymns.[1] Thus the redeemer is regularly designated the Word (ϣⲉϫⲉ, GT 16, 34; 23, 20 and 33 f.; 26, 5; 37, 7; λόγος, GT 37, 8 and 11); and one reads of him 'who came forth from him [*sc.* God] and who is himself' (GT 38, 8–10), which is reminiscent of John i. 1, θεὸς ἦν ὁ λόγος, and that 'nothing happens without him' (GT 37, 21 f.), which is parallel to John i. 3, χωρὶς αὐτοῦ ἐγένετο οὐδὲ ἕν. In GT 31, 13–16, light and life come from the mouth of the Son, which is certainly to be compared to John i, where the life, which is the light, is in the Word (*v.* 4); and the redeemer, as in John i. 12, comes to those who repent (GT 35, 20–2). Also, in GT 36, 11 f. the redeemer is the 'finding of the Light of Truth' which goes forth from him; and in GT 18, 17 Jesus illuminates those who are in obscurity. As in John i. 10, there are those who do not know their creator (GT 19, 10–14; 22, 27–33), and in 27, 22 f. we read of those who, 'although they are in him...do not know him', and again in 27, 31–3 of 'those who do not yet exist', that they 'are ignorant of him who has produced them'. There are some who do not receive a name (GT 21, 38 f.), and since the Name is so strongly linked to the redeemer in the Gospel of Truth (GT 38–41), this statement is perhaps similar to John i. 11, 'his own did not receive him'.[2] Certainly the opening of the Gospel of Truth (16, 31 ff.) is like John i. 12 when it says, 'The Gospel of Truth is joy for those who have *received* from the Father of Truth the *grace of knowing him* through the power of the Word, which has come from the πλήρωμα...he whom they call σωτήρ'. (Italics mine.) In GT 26, 4 ff. it is expressly said that the Word 'had become body (σῶμα)', and 31, 1 ff. reports that the 'hylics' did not see his form, 'for he came in a σάρξ of similitude'. This would appear to be an intentional corollary of John i. 14, where the community *did* see the glory of the Word become flesh.

In comparison with this last passage in the Gospel of Truth, it should also be noted that Phil. ii. 7, where Christ is in the *likeness* or *form* of man, presents a similar concept. Thus GT 20,

---

[1] The attempt of Cerfaux, 'De Saint Paul à "L'Évangile de la Vérité"', *NTS*, vol. v (1958/9), pp. 103–12, to explain the Gospel of Truth as a work consciously dependent on the first chapters of Romans is highly unconvincing.

[2] Cf. also John xvii. 6–12, where the disciples are kept in God's name.

28 f., in a way similar to Phil. ii. 8, says that Jesus abased himself unto death, and in GT 38, 11 f. the redeemer is given 'his
name, which belonged to him'. It is not clear here whose name
is given—whether the redeemer receives his own name, which
is now authentically his, or whether the redeemer receives the
name of the Father. At any rate, one should think of the naming
in Phil. ii. 9 ff., particularly when a few lines later one reads,
'before he had produced the Aeons, in order that the Name of
the Father might be over their heads, since it (or he) is *Lord*'
(GT 38, 35–8; italics mine).[1]

The words 'The Father of the All was ἀόρατος' (GT 20,
19 f.) are to be compared to Col. i. 15, as is GT 19, 5–10:
'that they may return to him [*sc.* to the Father, l. 3] and that
they may know him in a Knowledge, unique in its perfection,
him who produced the All and in whom the All existed and of
whom the All had need'. Here is the Nag Hammadi version of
the *Allmachtsformel*, and connected with it the idea of a return
of the All to the creator by means of the redeemer, Knowledge
(ⲥⲁⲩⲛⲉ). In GT 41, 28 f. the redeemer seems to be referred to as
the head of the redeemed; and in GT 23, 33–24, 7, where the
redeemer is named Word (ⲯⲉⲝⲉ), he evidences even stronger
similarities with the redeemer of Heb. i. 3: 'Thus the Word of
the Father goes forth from the All, being the fruit of his heart
and figure of his will. Yet he bears the All, he chooses them and,
even more, he puts on the form of the All, purifying it and
causing it to return to the Father...'[2] Here the words 'being
the fruit of his heart and the figure of his will. Yet he bears the
All...purifying it' are parallel to Heb. i. 3, ὢν ἀπαύγασμα τῆς
δόξης καὶ χαρακτὴρ τῆς ὑποστάσεως αὐτοῦ, φέρων τε τὰ
πάντα...καθαρισμὸν τῶν ἁμαρτιῶν ποιησάμενος.

In GT 20, 36–21, 2, the redeemer goes before those who have
been 'denuded by forgetfulness' and proclaims redemption to
them. This passage is thus reminiscent of I Pet. iii. 19, where
Christ is in the role of preaching to the spirits in bondage, and
of the ὤφθη ἀγγέλοις of I Tim. iii. 16.[3]

[1] Cf. also GT 39, 7–10.
[2] Cf. also GT 17, 4–6; 41, 13–19. Cf. further Giversen, 'Evangelium
Veritatis and the Epistle to the Hebrews', *Studia Theologica*, vol. XIII (1959),
pp. 87–96, who gives considerable attention to Heb. i. 1–5 but fails to note
the parallel between i. 3 and GT 23, 33 ff.
[3] Cf. also GT 22, 38 ff.; 24, 11–17.

The very close parallels, at times almost verbatim, between the Gospel of Truth and the New Testament Christological hymns, plus the dating of the Nag Hammadi materials over a lengthy period around the second century A.D.,[1] seem to point to the fact that the author of the Gospel of Truth was acquainted with the New Testament hymns. Certainly all the cosmological and theological concepts in the Gospel of Truth cannot be explained from the New Testament, however, and it appears that this work evidences the coming together of another tradition with the tradition stemming from the New Testament, particularly from the Christological hymns. As an example of the way in which this occurs, one may note GT 20, 10–21, 6. The discussion immediately preceding this passage has referred to a book of the Living which the redeemer is to take, perhaps reflecting the imagery of Revelation. Regarding the book it is said, 'No one among those who believed in salvation was able to become manifest as long as that book had not made its appearance' (GT 20, 6–9).[2] Then follows this passage:

For this reason Jesus the merciful and faithful patiently accepted the endurance of suffering until such time as he should have taken possession of that book, since he knew that his death meant life for many. Just as, so long as a testament has not been opened, the fortune of the deceased master of the house remains hidden, so too the All remained hidden as long as the Father of the All was invisible, since he is one in himself, from whom come forth all spaces. This is why Jesus appeared (and) clothed himself in that book. He was nailed to a cross;[3] he attached the deed of disposition of the

---

[1] Cf. van Unnik, *Evangelien aus dem Nilsand*, pp. 30 f. Of course some of the sources contained in them are older than others. The Apocryphon of John, for example, seems to be originally pre-Christian, the few Christianizing additions being transparent. Cf. also the Gospel of Philip, Logion 6 (Schenke, 'Das Evangelium nach Philippus', col. 6): '…when we were Hebrews'. Regarding the Christianizing of the redeemer tradition in the Coptic gnostic texts, cf. particularly Martin Krause, 'Das literarische Verhältnis des Eugnostosbriefes zur Sophia Jesu Christi. Zur Auseinandersetzung der Gnosis mit dem Christentum', *Mullus: Festschrift Theodor Klauser*, edd. Alfred Stuiber and Alfred Hermann (*JAC*, Ergänzungsband 1, 1964), pp. 215–23.

[2] Cf. Rev. xx. 15.

[3] The wooden rendering of ϣⲉ by all the translators as 'wood', perhaps because the Greek word σταυρός also occurs in the Gospel of Truth (20, 27), is needless, since ϣⲉ, which does indeed mean 'wood', is the regular Coptic word for σταυρός. Cf. W. E. Crum, *A Coptic Dictionary* (Oxford, 1939).

Father to the cross. O great teaching of such proportions! He abases himself even unto death though clothed with immortal life. Having divested himself of these perishable rags, he clothed himself in incorruptibility, which it is impossible for anyone to take away from him. Having penetrated into terror's empty spaces, he passed through those who were stripped by oblivion, having become both Knowledge and Perfection, proclaiming those (things) which are in the heart [. . .] to teach those [. . .]. But those who are to receive the teaching, [namely] the living who are inscribed in the book of the living, they receive the teaching for themselves alone.

The concept of the book here comes perhaps from Rev. v. 5 ff., and Jesus' acceptance of his suffering is similar to Phil. ii. 8, ἐταπείνωσεν ἑαυτόν. Also, that his death meant life for many may well be a reflection of Rom. iv. 25, 'who was handed over for our transgressions and was raised for our righteousness', which is in turn to be associated with I Tim. iii. 16, ὃς ἐφανερώθη ἐν σαρκί, ἐδικαιώθη ἐν πνεύματι, and I Pet. iii. 18, θανατωθεὶς μὲν σαρκί, ζωοποιηθεὶς δὲ πνεύματι. The reference to the opening of a will may be only an illustration drawn from the author's own environment;[1] but the 'attaching' of 'the deed of disposition of the Father to the cross' is probably drawn from Col. ii. 14, and that the Father of the All is ἀόρατος is likely to be explained from Col. i. 15.[2] Then follow other motifs which are also to be found in the various New Testament Christo- logical hymns; there is the *descensus ad inferos* and proclamation of salvation there, as in I Pet. iii. 19, and the community's receiving of the revelation, as in John i. 12–14.

Thus most of the elements in this passage may be explained as having come from the New Testament,[3] particularly from the New Testament Christological hymns, with some other elements

[1] Cf. no. Z338d of the Coptic 'Apophthegmata patrum Aegyptiorum' in Till, *Koptische Grammatik (saïdischer Dialekt)* (Leipzig, 1961), pp. 265 f.

[2] Although the invisibility of God is certainly a universal concept.

[3] Cf. van Unnik, 'The "Gospel of Truth" and the New Testament', *The Jung Codex*, ed. F. L. Cross (London, 1955), p. 122: 'It is clear that the writer of the *Gospel of Truth* was acquainted with the Gospels, the Pauline Epistles, Hebrews and Revelation...The author...knew these books and interpreted them in his own way.' With this one may agree; but it should be emphasized that this 'in his own way' should mean that the New Testament was correlated to a highly developed speculative system, not merely that the non-New Testament ideas in the Gospel of Truth are the result of someone's private meditation over the New Testament.

coming in that bear the stamp of cosmological and theological speculation from some other tradition. This situation, however, in which concepts in a given passage can be derived primarily from the New Testament, is precisely *not* true of the passage that immediately follows:

They receive it from the hand of the Father, (and) they turn anew towards him. Since the perfection of the All is in the Father, it is necessary for the All to reascend towards him. Therefore, if a person possesses the Knowledge, he takes that which is his own and he draws it to himself. For he who is ignorant is deficient, and it is a great deficiency, since it is that which ought to perfect him which he lacks. Since the perfection of the All is in the Father, it becomes necessary for the All to reascend towards him, (and) for each one to take possession of the things which are his own, which he registered in advance, having prepared them to be given to those who came from him. Those whose names he knew in advance were called at the end, so that he who knows is he whose name has been spoken by the Father. For he whose name has not been pronounced is ignorant (GT 21, 6–31).

Since it seems unlikely that the concepts presented in this speculative passage can be derived from the New Testament, it would seem to be justifiable to conclude that the Gospel of Truth attests the coming together of New Testament traditions[1] with other traditions.[2] This is probably the result of the coming of Christianity to a community in which such ideas as those found in GT 21, 6–31 were already prevalent,[3] as seems to be

[1] Since those redeemer concepts that are most like the New Testament are often related to the New Testament Christological hymns, this is perhaps evidence that the New Testament tradition first came to the community which produced the Gospel of Truth through the Christological hymns. Stated otherwise, perhaps the New Testament Christological hymns, or others similar to them, were known to that community before the other New Testament traditions.

[2] This does not mean that there are distinct literary sources in the Gospel of Truth. The author is probably merely composing out of his own background, and this composition at times leans heavily on that part of his background which is related to the New Testament, at times on that part of his background related to other traditions.

[3] A comparison between the Gospel of Truth and the Gospel of John has even led C. K. Barrett ('The Theological Vocabulary of the Fourth Gospel and of the Gospel of Truth', *Current Issues in New Testament Interpretation, Essays in honor of Otto A. Piper*, edd. William Klassen and Graydon F. Snyder (New York, 1962), p. 223) to assume a pre-Christian Gnosticism.

indicated by the fact that the Apocryphon of John is only Christianized by a few additions, primarily at the first, and that the Gospel of Philip refers to the time 'when we were Hebrews'.[1] This supposition seems to be further substantiated when, in the passage just quoted from the Gospel of Truth that is so strongly flavored with elements from the New Testament and in particular from the Christological hymns, one observes a few remarks that are more like the second passage, in which no New Testament influence is to be found, e.g. the All remains hidden, and 'spaces' emanate from the Father. This would seem to indicate that the author of the Gospel of Truth is interpreting New Testament material in the light of a separate tradition, or vice versa. The very strong association of the Gospel of Truth with the Odes of Solomon casts light on that separate tradition and its origin.

[1] Judaism certainly provided antecedents for much found in the Nag Hammadi literature, whether it is to be seen as the origin or matrix of the Nag Hammadi community or not. On the side of at least strong Jewish influence on emerging Gnosticism and on the community that produced the Nag Hammadi literature, cf. R. M. Grant, *Gnosticism and Early Christianity* (New York, 1959), particularly pp. 27 ff.; Otto Betz, *Der Paraklet* (Arbeiten zur Geschichte des Spätjudentums und Urchristentums, 2) (Leiden/ Cologne, 1963), pp. 221 f.; Betz, 'Was am Anfang geschah. Das jüdische Erbe in den neugefundenen koptisch-gnostischen Schriften', *Abraham Unser Vater. Juden und Christen im Gespräch über die Bibel, Festschrift für Otto Michel*, edd. Betz, *et al.* (Arbeiten..., 5) (Leiden/Cologne, 1963), pp. 24–43; and Nock, Review of *Gnosis und spätantiker Geist, Teil I*, by Hans Jonas, pp. 606–8. R. McL. Wilson employs the phrase, 'medium of Judaism' (Wilson, 'Gnosis, Gnosticism and the New Testament', *Le origini dello Gnosticismo. Colloquio di Messina* (Studies in the History of Religions (Supplements to *Numen*), 12), ed. Ugo Bianchi (Leiden, 1967), p. 524). Cf. further the literature on this issue given in n. 3 of the same page.
Hans Jonas, 'Response to G. Quispel's "Gnosticism and the New Testament"', *The Bible in Modern Scholarship. Papers Read at the 100th Meeting of the Society of Biblical Literature*, ed. J. Philip Hyatt (Nashville and New York, 1965), pp. 286–93, argues vigorously against Judaism's being the origin of Gnosticism, but also concurs in seeing Jewish antecedents. (The contrast 'origins/antecedents' is Jonas', *ibid.* p. 287.) Further evidence for Jonas' position is offered, in some detail, by Alexander Böhlig, 'Der jüdische und judenchristliche Hintergrund in gnostischen Texten von Nag Hammadi', *Le origini dello Gnosticismo*, pp. 109–40. Cf. further the following papers in the same volume: Grant, 'Les êtres intermédiaires dans le judaïsme tardif', pp. 141–54; Helmer Ringgren, 'Qumran and Gnosticism', pp. 379–84 (and the discussion of this paper on pp. 384–8); Menahem Mansoor, 'The Nature of Gnosticism in Qumran', pp. 389–400; and the 'Addenda et Postscripta' given by Wilson, pp. 691–7.

Hans-Martin Schenke, in his monograph entitled *Die Herkunft des sogenannten Evangelium Veritatis*,[1] has discussed this relationship and has substantiated it by references to the Odes of Solomon in footnotes to his translation of the Gospel of Truth.[2] It will serve our purpose here to call attention to those passages where the parallelism is strongest. First, one should note that Error (πλάνη) and Truth are hypostases in the Gospel of Truth, and that one represents the anti-divine power(s), the other the divine. Thus, in the opening section of the Gospel of Truth dealing with the primordial emanations, it is said of Error that 'it elaborated its own matter in emptiness, without knowing Truth. It applied itself to the modeling of a creature (πλάσμα), trying to provide in power (and) in beauty the equivalent of Truth' (GT 17, 15–21); and that 'Oblivion, (born) of Error, was not revealed' (17, 36 f.). Thus it is Error that persecutes and crucifies Christ (GT 18, 21 ff.),[3] who was teaching the way of Truth (GT 18, 20). With such passages are to be compared Ode Sol. xv. 6, 'The way of Error I have left'; xviii. 10, 'Error thou knowest not, for neither doth it know thee'; xxxi. 2, 'Error went astray, and (perished) from him'; and particularly xxxviii. 6–10:

Error fled away from him
and would not meet him,

But Truth was proceeding in the right way,
and whatever I did not know he[4] made clear to me:

All the drugs of Error
and the (allurements which are considered the sweetness of Death).

And I saw the destroyer of the corruptor [or: the destroyer of destruction]...

And I asked the Truth, Who are these? And he said to me...[5]

---

[1] Schenke, *Die Herkunft des sogenannten Evangelium Veritatis* (Göttingen, 1959).

[2] Cf. particularly *ibid.* pp. 25–9.   [3] Cf. I Cor. ii. 8.

[4] ‏ܠܝܪܐ‎, of course, is feminine. This use of the masculine is perhaps to be explained by the association in the Odes of Solomon of Truth with the odist, or the Petgama, or both. Bauer, *Die Oden Salomos*, however, assumes a mistake and translates 'she'.

[5] Cf. *v.* 1: 'I went up into the Light of Truth as into a chariot; and the Truth led me.'

'Father of Truth', of course (GT 16, 33), is a term familiar from Ode Sol. xli. 9. When GT 26, 34–27, 4 then says, 'Truth is the mouth of the Father; his tongue is the Holy Spirit. Whoever attaches himself to Truth attaches himself to the mouth of the Father by his [i.e. the Father's] tongue when he receives the Holy Spirit', one should recall Ode Sol. xii. 3, 'The mouth of the Lord is the Word (which is true)', and the identification of Word and Truth in Ode Sol. xxxii. 2. When the redeemer enlightens 'those who were in darkness' and 'indicated a path' which is Truth (GT 18, 17 ff.), this recalls Ode Sol. xi. 3, where the odist says that he ran 'in the way of Truth'; and Ode Sol. xxiii. 5, 'his Will descended from on high', is perhaps a forerunner of GT 37, 4 ff., where the Will is an hypostasis connected with emanations.

Also, the figure of the Father's breasts, in some way related to the Son and the Spirit (Ode Sol. xix. 2–4), is seen in GT 24, 9 ff.: 'The Father reveals his breast, but his breast is the Holy Spirit. He reveals that of himself which was hidden; that of himself which was hidden is his Son.' To be sure, other parallels can be drawn between the Gospel of Truth and the Odes of Solomon,[1] but the more important of those that are related to the *other* tradition which comes together with the New Testament tradition in the Gospel of Truth have been observed.[2]

Thus the Gospel of Truth apparently shows how New Testament concepts, particularly Christological formulations highly similar to the New Testament Christological hymns, could be linked to an already well developed speculative gnostic—or 'gnosticizing'—system. When precisely this system

---

[1] Cf. Schenke, *Die Herkunft des sogenannten Evangelium Veritatis.* Some of the parallels are weak, but the evidence is strong enough to show that we are dealing with the same tradition. Schenke's argument has convinced at least Schulz, 'Salomo-Oden', col. 1341. Grant, 'Notes on Gnosis', *VChr*, vol. xi (1957), pp. 149–51, also compares the Gospel of Truth with the Odes of Solomon. Cf. further F.-M. Braun, 'L'énigme des Odes de Solomon', *Revue Thomiste*, vol. LVII (1957), p. 611, and Braun, *Jean le théologien et son évangile dans l'Église ancienne* (Paris, 1959), p. 237.

[2] Eric Segelberg, 'Evangelium Veritatis—a confirmation homily and its relation to the Odes of Solomon', *Orientalia Suecana*, vol. VIII (1959), pp. 17–41, lists a number of motifs in the Gospel of Truth (which he considers related to sacraments) not to be found in the Odes of Solomon. That is quite in keeping, however, with the kind of conceptual relatedness suggested here.

can be rather closely related to the Odes of Solomon, that would seem to lend further support to the thesis that the leading ideas of the Odes of Solomon have their origin outside the New Testament tradition, and thus indirectly to substantiate the view that the Odes of Solomon and the New Testament Christological hymns share a common matrix.

THE APOCALYPSE OF ADAM

If the Gospel of Truth apparently brings together New Testament tradition and another tradition which is mythological and speculative, this is only slightly true for the Apocryphon of John and not at all true for the Apocalypse of Adam. Although the Apocryphon of John exhibits specifically Christian traits in places—the name of Christ that appears several times and the 'Christianizing' prologue (19, 6–20, 3)[1]—the myth it recounts is otherwise lacking in Christian elements. Like most gnostic documents, it seems to reveal an extensive eclecticism; yet it is heavily Jewish. The passage beginning at 47, 15 is in fact a commentary, from the gnostic viewpoint, on the creation stories of Genesis. Characteristic of this 'gnosticizing' of the Old Testament is the statement 'Elohim is the Righteous, Yahwe is the Unrighteous' (62, 13–15). This prominence of Old Testament allusions and motifs in the Apocryphon of John and the seemingly secondary Christian elements lead one toward the conclusion that the community producing it was Jewish before it was Christian, although it cannot at present be said whether that community was originally Jewish and adopted Gnosticism, or originally gnostic and adopted the Old Testament.

Far less complex in its mythology than the Apocryphon of John, and lacking in Christian elements, is the Apocalypse of Adam. The Old Testament element is prominent here throughout. The apocalypse is that received by Adam and passed on to his son Seth; Eva is mentioned as Seth's mother, and Adam says that they were like the angels (64, 14 f.); they served God in fear and servitude (65, 20 f., *et passim*); the spirit of life is blown into them (66, 21–3); they fall (67, 1–9); Noah and his sons

[1] References are to Berolinensis 8502 (cf. p. 121 n. 2). On the 'Christian framework' of the Apocryphon of John, cf. further Wilson, 'Gnosis, Gnosticism and the New Testament', p. 512 n. 2.

become part of the drama (70, 17 ff.); there is a promised land to which the chosen are to come (72, 3–7)—to mention only some of the more prominent Old Testament motifs in the work.

In the midst of this work, which draws so strongly on the Old Testament and which seems to show no Christian influence at all, there appears the myth of a redeemer in many ways similar to the myth present in the New Testament Christological hymns. This redeemer is named Φωστήρ, Enlightener (76, 9 ff.). As the whole πλάσμα (76, 17) is under the power of death, he redeems men from death (76, 15); and he overcomes the (evil) powers and archons (77, 2) and attains a position more exalted than theirs (77, 7). It is here emphasized that the powers do not see the *Phōstēr* (77, 14). In a passage referred to by Böhlig as an 'excursus' (77, 27–83, 4), there occur fourteen statements, each briefly describing the birth and coming of the redeemer, where it is each time said that he 'received glory and power'. Particularly to be noted is 78, 15 f., 'Arise, God has glorified you'. As Böhlig notes,[1] this series of similar statements is apparently a syncretistic method, whereby varying redeemer myths are coordinated. The enlightenment given by the *Phōstēr*, finally, passes, via those who have received his enlightenment, to the whole aeon (83, 1–4).

In his introduction to the text and translation of the work, Böhlig suggested that the 'supposition of a pre-Christian concept' was much closer to the accurate explanation of the *Phōstēr* in the Apocalypse of Adam than the supposition of Christian influence.[2] This opinion has been echoed by Kurt Rudolph[3] and George W. MacRae.[4] Böhlig suggested Zoroastrianism as the nearest parallel to the *Phōstēr*[5] and considered the work to be probably the result of 'a comparison between Jewish Gnosticism and Iranian concepts'.[6] In this, also, he was followed by Rudolph.[7] MacRae thinks the work may be 'a sort of Gnostic midrash built on the Deutero-Isaian Servant Songs',[8]

[1] Böhlig, *Koptisch-gnostische Apokalypsen aus Codex V von Nag Hammadi*, p. 92.
[2] *Ibid.* p. 90.
[3] Rudolph, review of *Koptisch-gnostische Apokalypsen aus Codex V von Nag Hammadi*, *ThLZ*, vol. xc (1965), cols. 361 f.
[4] George W. MacRae, 'The Coptic Gnostic Apocalypse of Adam', *Heythrop Journal*, vol. vi (1965), pp. 31–5.   [5] Böhlig, pp. 90 f.   [6] *Ibid.* p. 91.
[7] Rudolph, review of *Koptisch-gnostische Apokalypsen aus Codex V von Nag Hammadi*, col. 362.   [8] MacRae, p. 33.

but, as was seen above in Part 2, the canonical Isaiah *itself* can hardly account for such a myth, and the *Phōstēr* of the Apocalypse of Adam would hardly remind anyone acquainted with the Iranian mythology and its emphasis on light of the Servant Songs of Deutero-Isaiah. Böhlig points especially to the redemptive activity of the Iranian Sošyan, who 'destroys evil, establishes a realm of righteousness, and raises the dead'.[1]

One will note that the *Phōstēr* of the Apocalypse of Adam seems not to have participated in creation, nor does he enter human existence in the way the Christ of the New Testament Christological hymns does. Precisely these observations, however, add more weight to the argument that the Apocalypse of Adam is uninfluenced by Christianity. Thus the Apocalypse of Adam provides yet another—perhaps the clearest—example of how Jewish motifs could mingle with redeemer concepts from other religions in the context of emerging Gnosticism *prior* to influence from Christianity. The published texts from Nag Hammadi seem therefore to make it clear, although they were written after the beginning of the Christian era, that some segments of Judaism—or religious groups under strong, even primary influence from Judaism—did in fact appropriate a redeemer myth—indeed, apparently a variety of redeemer myths—apart from any influence from Christianity. That the Nag Hammadi texts are not tied so closely and exclusively to Jewish Wisdom speculation merely shows that this appropriation took place not only at one time and place, but over a period of time in various parts of the eastern Mediterranean world. If they do not bear directly on the background of the New Testament Christological hymns, the Nag Hammadi texts show that it was entirely possible for the myth found in those hymns to have been given by the Jewish environment of early Christianity. Thus, rather than arguing that the redeemer motifs of the Odes of Solomon and of the Nag Hammadi texts stem from the New Testament, it would seem more appropriate to conclude that the three groups—New Testament Christological hymns, Nag Hammadi texts (especially the Apocalypse of Adam), and the Odes of Solomon—represent a more or less parallel development of concepts infiltrating the various religions of the eastern Mediterranean world around the beginning of the Christian era.

[1] Böhlig, p. 90.

CHAPTER 8

THE THANKSGIVINGS OF THE WISDOM SCHOOL

In an essay in the Rowley *Festschrift* entitled 'Psalms and Wisdom',[1] Sigmund Mowinckel has provided a description of that matrix from which the New Testament Christological hymns may be seen to stem. In this essay Mowinckel maintains the thesis that in 'late Jewish psalmography...we have to do with a psalmography that has originated in the circles of the "wise men", the learned leaders of the "wisdom schools"'.[2] He begins by pointing out that psalm poetry originated in the temple cult, but that there are some psalms in the psalter which appear to be private rather than cultic. How did they come to be included in the collection? Mowinckel's answer is that they were used by teachers of the 'wisdom school' for didactic purposes.[3] 'From of old these "learned" or "wise" men used to cultivate a special kind of literature, "the poetry of wisdom", which was cultivated all over the Orient, and had a common, markedly international, character, in Egypt, Babylonia and Canaan.'[4] The form (proverbs, pithy sayings) of wisdom poetry has marked many of the psalms of the psalter, and the influence of its substance is also felt there. 'This becomes apparent for instance in the testimonies of the thanksgiving psalms and their exhortations to the congregation, in which the tone, in the nature of the case, is didactic. Naturally these passages will have the form of a "proverb", a wise saying.'[5]

According to Mowinckel, one may not only observe, at an early stage, the effect of wisdom poetry on the poetry of the psalter, but one may also see that, at a later date, the learned

---

[1] Sigmund Mowinckel, 'Psalms and Wisdom', *Wisdom in Israel and in the Ancient Near East*, pp. 205–25.

[2] *Ibid.* p. 206.

[3] The association of the name Solomon with wisdom literature refers 'probably' to his being 'the one who founded the school for scribes in Jerusalem and introduced there the international poetry of wisdom of the Orient' (*ibid.* p. 206).

[4] *Ibid.* p. 207.   [5] *Ibid.* p. 208.

men who were the scribes became themselves psalmists,[1] and consequently 'to the ancient cultic poetry was added a later, private, learned psalmography'. Writers of such psalms 'were men of prayers', and 'officially inspired "*pneumatics*". To be able to pray rightly, to make a doxology or a prayer with the proper content and in the proper form, was considered not only evidence of piety, but also proof of the inspiration which the wise claimed for themselves and were conscious of possessing (Sir. xiv. 10; xxxix. 5 f.).[2]

The chief vehicle which the wisdom poets adopted for conveying their teaching was the *thanksgiving* psalm. Here the experience of personal salvation could become a didactic principle.

When now in the thanksgiving psalms the experience is expressed in a general sentence (Ps. xxxvii. 35 f.), or in the form of a blessing (Ps. xxxii. 1 f.), or through direct admonition in the imperative (Ps. xxxiv. 4–9), or by inviting others to take a lesson from what has been (Ps. xxxiv. 12 ff.), all this is a result of influence from the poetry of wisdom. Consequently the thanksgiving psalm may become chiefly instructive and approximate to the didactic poem, as is the case with Ps. xxxiv.[3]

'It is', then, 'this learned, non-cultic psalmography which is followed up by the post-canonical, late Jewish psalmography.'[4] This includes, aside from 'legendary stories', psalmody in Sirach and in the Psalms of Solomon. 'The thanksgiving psalm of Sirach (li. 1–12), evidently on a concrete occasion, has a... personal note: that of thanking for the help of God in the dangers to which the calumny of mighty enemies had exposed him.'[5]

[1] Mowinckel's thesis, in spite of differences of opinion that may still exist among members of the Old Testament community, may be considered to have been generally accepted. Georg Fohrer (*Einleitung in das Alte Testament*, p. 320) concludes his discussion of 'Collections and Origin of the Psalter' with the following statement: 'It may not be overlooked that Ps. i, finally placed at the front of the whole [corpus], presents a Wisdom song. Thereby was the psalter taken out of its life in worship, divorced from its original *Sitz im Leben* and from that of many of the songs collected in it, and fixed as a book of edification for Wisdom theology.'

[2] Mowinckel, pp. 208, 210. Cf. also Sir. xlii. 15 ff.; xxxix. 12 ff.; li. 1 ff.

[3] *Ibid.* p. 214.   [4] *Ibid.* p. 217.

[5] *Ibid.* p. 218.

Instead of this personal element, the Psalms of Solomon reflect the national tragedy centering around and following the fall of Maccabean rule, and

in the thanksgiving psalm xiii, the political events are re-echoed; the poet thanks God because he has been saved from the catastrophe that has befallen the sinners. Contrary to the classical psalms, the poet speaks more of the fall of his antagonists, the 'sinners', than of his own salvation; cf., however, Ps. lxxiii. Here the didactic style is obvious.[1]

In these didactic thanksgiving psalms, the '*eschatological hope*' is prominent. It is still, however, 'in the old nationalistic-political intramundane form. Ps. Sol. xvii is built up after the pattern of the psalm of lamentation and supplication. It starts with the confession of faith in "the Lord, our king for ever"'; then follows the lament, which finally leads to 'the prayer: "Behold, O Lord, and raise up unto them their king, the son of David, at the time which Thou seest that he may reign over Israel Thy servant!" The prayer includes a long description of the blessings that Messiah will bring to his people, and ends with the confidence of being heard.'[2] Thus, in this extra-canonical psalmography, disaster and hope for the future are the most prominent features.

From the milieu of this psalmography of the Wisdom school apparently stem both the New Testament Christological hymns[3] and at least some of the Odes of Solomon. Again it is Col. i. 12–20 that, because of the preservation of its *thanksgiving* form, reveals the connection. When this thanksgiving offers thanks (*v.* 13) for 'deliverance from the dominion of darkness', it immediately recalls the thanksgiving in Sir. li, where one reads, 'I sent up my supplication from the earth, and prayed for deliverance from death' (*v.* 9), after which comes the conclusion,

---

[1] *Ibid.* pp. 219 f.   [2] *Ibid.* p. 221.

[3] The question of whether or not individual hymns are pre-Christian thus becomes relatively unimportant; for the historical religious matrix would have provided both form and matter, and Christianity might take over and adapt some hymns (or not adapt them), while creating others on the same pattern. The presence of such terms as cross and church, already recognized on formal grounds to be additions to the original hymns, thus stamps the individual hymns as being *exclusively* Christian, i.e. no longer appropriate for use in the non-Christian Wisdom school.

> I will praise thy name continually,
>   and will sing praise with thanksgiving.
>
> .   .   .   .
>
> For thou didst save me from destruction
>   and rescue me from an evil plight.
> Therefore I will give thanks to thee and praise thee
>   and I will bless the name of the Lord
>
> (Sir. li. 11 f.)

If the developing myth which has concerned us here is not present in this thanksgiving, it certainly is elsewhere in Sirach, as has already been seen in several places. Thus it may be suggested that the New Testament Christological hymns had their formal matrix within the Wisdom school, and this of course coincides with the thesis that they represent a stage of a developing myth which had its prior development in Wisdom speculation.[1]

Certain of the Odes of Solomon also belong within the corpus of thanksgiving hymns of the Wisdom school. The clearest example is Ode v,

> I (thank thee, Lord,
>   for) I love thee (v. 1).

The hymn that follows is then a statement of trust that the Lord will save or keep the odist from his persecutors. The relevant word occurs again in Ode Sol. xxvi. 5 f.,

> (From the East to the West
>   the praise is his,
>
> And from the South to the North
>   his is the thanksgiving)[2] (ﬂﬂﬂ = Hebrew תּוֹדָה).

The most significant occurrence of the word, however, is at the conclusion of Ode vii, which is the one Ode that is materially closest to the New Testament Christological hymns:

---

[1] Deichgräber, pp. 145 f., has argued strongly against considering the hymn of Col. i. 15–20—and by implication the other New Testament Christological hymns as well—to be a thanksgiving. His argument that a thanksgiving is inappropriate to such a Christological hymn (*ibid.* p. 146) is difficult to understand; cf. below, ch. 9. Here, it would seem that Deichgräber has failed to take sufficient account of the argument of Robinson, 'Die Hodajot-Formel in Gebet und Hymnus des Frühchristentums'.

[2] Rendered 'confession' by the translators.

As (the course of anger against) evil,
   so is the (course of joy toward what is) beloved,
   and brings in of its fruits without restraint.

My joy is the Lord and my (course) is toward him.
   This (my way is lovely),

For (it is my helper) to the Lord.
   He (has caused me to know himself), without grudging,
      in his (magnanimity),
   (for) his kindness (made his greatness small).

He became like me, (in order) that I might receive him,
   (he appeared in likeness as myself, in order) that I might
      put him on.

And I trembled not when I saw him,
   (for he is my grace).

Like my nature he became, (in order) that I might learn him,
   and like my (appearance, in order) that I might not turn
      back from him.

The father of knowledge
   is the word of knowledge.

He who created Wisdom
   is wiser than his works.

And he who created me when yet I was not
   knew what I (would) do when I came into being.

(For this cause) he pitied me in his abundant (mercy)
   (and granted to me that I might pray him and would)
      receive from his sacrifice.

For he (is imperishable),
   (fulness of the worlds and their father).

He (gave himself to be seen by those who) are his,
   (in order that they should know him who) made them
   and that they (should not think) that they came of them-
      selves.

For (he established to knowledge its) way,
   (made it wide and long) and brought it to all perfection.

And he set over it the traces of his light,
  and (it runs from beginning to) end.

For by him (it was wrought),
  and he was pleased with the Son.

And (for its) salvation he will take (hold) of everything,
  and the Most High shall be known (among his Holy Ones),

.   .   .   .

For (he) hath given a mouth to his creation,
  to open the voice of the mouth towards him (and for his
  praise).

Confess (ܐܘܕܐ) (his power and make known) his grace.

Although the word ܐܘܕܐ must be translated 'confess' here and
not 'thank', and although the standard thanksgiving formula
is not employed, still one sees that, precisely where the myth of
the redeemer in the Odes of Solomon most nearly approximates
the myth of the New Testament Christological hymns, there the
word for thanking appears. Since both Ode Sol. xxvi. 5 f. and
Sir. li. 12 make thanking and praising parallel, and since the
Odes frequently call for the praise of the Lord or of the Most
High,[1] one probably should cite the numerous instances of
praising (root ܫܒܚ) in the Odes of Solomon as further evidence
of the relation of the Odes to the thanksgivings of the Wisdom
school.

The Nag Hammadi literature is not rich in thanksgivings,
which would seem to indicate that the cultic setting for this
literature was different from that of the New Testament
Christological hymns and of the Odes of Solomon. The
Apocalypse of Adam, however, does contain a hymn of sorts,
which begins,

Hail to the soul of every man,
  for they have known God with a Gnosis of truth
                                                    (83, 11–14).

---

[1] Particularly to be noted is Ode Sol. xxvi. 1 f., where the word 'praise'
replaces the word 'thank' in the regular thanksgiving formula:

ܐܘܕܐ ܠܡܪܝܐ ܡܛܠ ܕܐܢܐ
ܕܝܠܗ ...

Cf. Ode Sol. v. 1:   ܐܘܕܐ ܠܟ ܡܪܝܐ ܡܛܠ ܕܐܢܐ
ܕܝܠܗ ...

138

Also, Apocryphon of John 35, 13–16 offers this clear example:

> I honor and praise thy invisible spirit,
>   for because of thee have all things come to be,
>   and all things (strive?) toward thee.

The Coptic gnostic literature therefore seems to give evidence of at least some reminiscence of the connection between thanksgiving hymns and the developing gnostic myth.

The Wisdom circles of Judaism, then, where the thanksgiving hymn was most at home, seem to have provided the most convenient point of entry for redeemer motifs from other religions into Judaism, or to have provided the best possibility of a merger.[1] The New Testament Christological hymns reflect one stage in this process, at which time the aspect of cosmic redemption was added to the role of the variously named mythical being of Judaism, as has been discussed. Some Christians then found this stage of the developing myth appropriate for an explanation of the Christ event. The Coptic gnostic materials from Nag Hammadi reveal a considerably more advanced stage of this process of syncretism, at which time the connection with Wisdom groups has been entirely left behind—although of course Sophia continues to play a prominent role in the various myths—the process now either becoming or merging with a new and distinct religion, Gnosticism. The Odes of Solomon belong to some stage of the syncretistic process intermediate to the New Testament and the Nag Hammadi materials, but independent of the New Testament and showing in several respects a less advanced stage of the developing redeemer myth.

---

[1] One will recall that the Dead Sea Scrolls now offer proof of the influence of Iranian dualism on Judaism, although the redeemer motif is here excluded.

CHAPTER 9

THE NEW TESTAMENT
CHRISTOLOGICAL HYMNS
AS LANGUAGE

The current discussion about New Testament hermeneutic[1] provides an insight for understanding the use of these hymns by Christianity prior to their inclusion in New Testament writings. Apparently, not a single one of the hymns has survived in its original form,[2] a fact which points to the early necessity for interpreting the hymns, to their inability to bear the full content of meaning read into them at a prior time, or read out of them, or which one hoped they would bear. They express the gospel, yet they do not express the gospel quite adequately; thus certain emendations are considered necessary by the New Testament writers in using the hymns. This observation, however, is at the same time an observation about all of language. All of language is not quite adequate for bearing the meaning one hopes it will bear; thus, it is always necessary to emend, to explain, to interpret, to 'translate'. Another way of saying this is to say that speech is bounded by silence.[3] One understands

---

[1] For the uninitiated, an excellent introduction to this discussion is *The New Hermeneutic*, edd. James M. Robinson and John B. Cobb, Jr (New Frontiers in Theology, 2) (New York, 1964), especially the introductory essay by Robinson (pp. 1–77).

[2] One may object that at least I Tim. iii. 16 has survived in the original. The comparison with I Pet. iii. 18–22, however, renders this assumption suspect.

[3] For this and many of the ideas in this chapter, I am indebted to Robert W. Funk, *Language, Hermeneutic, and Word of God. The Problem of Language in the New Testament and Contemporary Theology* (New York and Evanston, 1966), particularly ch. ix. Samuel Laeuchli, *The Language of Faith. An Introduction to the Semantic Dilemma of the Early Church* (New York and Nashville, 1962), also deals admirably with this issue, although the discussion is focused on second-century Christianity. Cf. in particular pp. 238–40. The slogan with which Laeuchli closes his book is most apt: *lingua semper reformanda*. Cf. further Deichgräber, p. 206, who affirms, 'Every language, every word, every formulation is less than that of which it speaks and which it formulates'. In his work, Funk draws heavily on the work of recent

the meaning conveyed by what is spoken as much by what is not said as by what is said. This silence, however, calls for articulation; the meaning conveyed by what is not said seeks to come to expression; hence, interpretation, 'translation' into different categories, application to certain situations.

The silence bounding speech and yearning toward articulation, however, immediately poses the problem of understanding —that is, there is no guarantee that the silence, the total meaning seeking expression in the particular 'language-gesture',[1] will receive a uniform understanding. In fact, it is almost certain *not* to receive uniform understanding. Consequently, what is virtually the same myth, from the same religious milieu, from the same linguistic (liturgical) context, occurring at various times and places as a particular instance of articulation, receives a variety of interpretations and applications from the several New Testament writers. It is fallacious to say that the New Testament writers misunderstood the myth, misinterpreted the linguistic occurrence of the thanksgiving hymn, or that only one interpreted it correctly while the others did not. To the contrary, they all understood, they all heard the silence bounding the hymn speaking. Had they not, they could not have emended the hymns, could not have applied them each in his own way; they probably would not have quoted the hymns at all. The new articulation, however—the interpretation, the 'translation' that seeks to render intelligible not only what was said in the hymn but what was not said as well—is determined by the interpreter's 'linguistic perspective'.[2] He may be conscious of this linguistic perspective or not conscious of it; he may be aware that he is using language calculated to cause his readers (or hearers) to stand where he stood when he first understood the hymn, or he may naïvely assume that his reformulation is 'final', that he has rendered the meaning conveyed to him only in silence forever into articulation. Whichever is the case, his interpretation seeks to insure the transmission to others of the meaning he originally received via the hymn.

If one sets aside the task of explicating each writer's inter-

phenomenologists of language, especially Maurice Merleau-Ponty (*Signs*, trans. R. C. McCleary (Evanston, 1964)).

[1] Funk, p. 237 *et passim*.   [2] *Ibid.* p. 226.

pretation of the myth in his particular thanksgiving hymn—a task better left to commentaries and for which an historical religious investigation is unnecessary once it is realized that the writer is quoting and interpreting prior material—and turns instead to an attempt to understand the function of the hymns as they were employed before the necessity was felt further to interpret them, one is to some degree on less certain ground. One is on less certain ground because it is not absolutely known whether the thanksgiving hymns were an original language-gesture or were themselves commentaries on a prior language-gesture or gestures, and if so what that prior language-gesture was and what meaning it sought to convey. One is *only to some degree* on less certain ground, however, because it is not unknown in what milieu the hymns would originally have been most meaningful and from what milieu they came. The historical religious analysis has shown that: Jewish Wisdom schools, where the thanksgiving was the vehicle for the transmission of knowledge and where the myth already discussed at length was developing toward the stage revealed in the New Testament Christological hymns. This knowledge of the milieu in which the hymns originally had their setting allows one to pose the question, What did these hymns, as appropriated (or composed) by Christianity, seek to convey; what was their linguistic function? and to be able to answer that question with at least a good degree of probability.

It is a presupposition here that the earliest *kerygma* of Christianity was of the crucifixion and resurrection of Jesus, and in those terms. This was the gospel, the 'good news' carried by the first Christian preachers. It should be clear, however, that such a message is not in and of itself good news; rather, the meaning conveyed by means of this proclamation is good news. The earliest *kerygma* served as a pipe line through which the water of life flowed to the hearers. That means, however, that, just as was the case with the New Testament writers' use of the Christological hymns, so here meaning was conveyed by what was not said as well as by what was said; the earliest articulation of the *kerygma* was itself bounded by silence which, like all silence bounding speech, called for articulation. This universal phenomenon of language may be presupposed even for the earliest proclamation of the gospel.

The recipient of the good news responds by thanking God, or by blessing or glorifying or magnifying God.[1] When the good news comes in the form of a direct confrontation with the power of God present in Jesus, the recipient gives thanks to Jesus (Luke xvii. 16); and when the good news comes by anticipation in the sure sign of the birth of John, Zechariah responds with a blessing, the formal alternate to the thanksgiving,

> Blessed be the Lord God of Israel,
> for he has visited and redeemed his people
> (Luke i. 68—RSV).

Comparably, the blind man who receives his sight 'glorifies' God (Luke xviii. 43), the eunuch baptized by Philip 'rejoices' (Acts viii. 39), and Cornelius and his household 'magnify' God (Acts x. 46). The person who was accustomed to formulating thanksgivings would certainly have thanked upon receiving the good news; nor would his thanking have been limited to the moment of receiving. Certainly the need to thank God repeatedly would have been felt. The conjecture may now be ventured that, when the gospel was received by persons accustomed to forming or singing the type of thanksgiving hymn of which the New Testament Christological hymns are examples, the myth expressed in these hymns provided a 'linguistic perspective' for understanding and appropriating the meaning of the gospel; the silence bounding the original gospel message sought expression for such persons in the myth of redemption with which they were familiar. As persons from such circles became converts to Christianity, the impulse to thank God would almost certainly have assured their carrying the content of their previous thanksgivings into their new, Christian thanksgivings. One may say that, in the experience of such persons, the thanksgiving hymn as 'spoken' word became once again 'speaking' word, i.e. the thanksgivings suddenly took on new meaning, suddenly received a relevance and implied an immediacy not present before.

It is significant to note that the thanksgiving did not remain

[1] On this issue, cf. further Deichgräber's stimulating concluding chapter on 'Theologische Erwägungen zum Lobpreis der frühen Christenheit' (Deichgräber, pp. 197–214). Understood broadly, it is not too much when he says (*ibid.* p. 214), 'In praising alone does man fulfill God's will'.

in the realm of response to God for receipt of the good news, did not remain a linguistic response that merely clarified for oneself and received clarification for itself, did not become 'speaking' word only for the one by whom it was now seen as having been previously only 'spoken' word. Precisely the thanksgiving hymn became a language-gesture seeking to convey meaning to the non-Christian. Paul admonished the Corinthians,

If I pray in a tongue, my spirit prays but my mind is unfruitful. What am I to do? I will pray with the spirit and I will pray with the mind also; I will sing with the spirit and I will sing with the mind also. Otherwise, if you bless with the spirit, how can any one in the position of an outsider say the 'Amen' to your thanksgiving when he does not know what you are saying? For you may give thanks well enough, but the other man is not edified

(I Cor. xiv. 14–17—RSV).[1]

It is clear that Paul calls here for the thanksgiving to be proclamation, and one may probably assume that others were of the same mind. That not all thanksgivings were gibberish is of course obvious from the presence in the New Testament of the Christological hymns. It seems, then, that the thanksgiving hymn, as it was originally used in Christianity, having received the clarification provided it by the gospel, attempted to express in then current language the meaning of the *kerygma*. Whether such an attempt could ever have been made employing solely the hymn, without some words of interpretation, cannot be known; it does not, however, seem likely.

Between I Cor. xiv. 14–17 and Phil. ii. 6–11 the thanksgiving comes full cycle. Discovered to be an appropriate language-gesture for bearing the meaning of the gospel, its content must then be further interpreted and applied. At one time and place, the thanksgiving Christological hymns said better and more fully, more adequately, what the gospel intended to say. Quickly, however, it was realized that even these language-gestures were bounded by still more silence; and it was now calling for articulation. As the New Testament Christological hymns appear in the New Testament writings, the meaning once conveyed by them is yearning toward, and receiving, further articulation.

[1] The words 'pray', 'sing', 'bless', and 'thank' are of course to be recognized as synonymous.

BIBLIOGRAPHY

Baudissin, Wolf Wilhelm. *Adonis und Esmun*. Leipzig, 1911.
Studien zur semitischen Religionsgeschichte, vol. II. Leipzig, 1878.
Beer, Georg. 'Pseudepigraphen des AT.s; II. A: Die Psalmen und Oden Salomos.' *PRE*, vol. XXIV. Ed. Albert Hauck. Leipzig, 1913³.
'Salomo-Oden.' *Paulys Real-Encyclopädie der classischen Altertumswissenschaft*, 2. Reihe, vol. I, 2. Edd. Wilhelm Kroll and Kurt Witte. Stuttgart, 1920.
Bornkamm, Günther. 'Das Bekenntnis im Hebräerbrief.' *Studien zu Antike und Urchristentum, Gesammelte Aufsätze*, vol. II. Beiträge zur Evangelischen Theologie, 28. Munich, 1959.
'Zum Verständnis des Christus-Hymnus Phil. 2, 6–11.' *Studien zu Antike und Urchristentum, Gesammelte Aufsätze*, vol. II. Beiträge zur Evangelischen Theologie, 28. Munich, 1959.
Bultmann, Rudolf. 'Die Bedeutung der neuerschlossenen mandäischen und manichäischen Quellen für das Verständnis des Johannesevangeliums.' *ZNW*, vol. XXIV. 1925.
'Bekenntnis- und Liedfragmente im ersten Petrusbrief.' *Coniectanea Neotestamentica*, vol. XI. 1947.
Das Evangelium des Johannes. Kritisch-exegetischer Kommentar über das Neue Testament. Göttingen, 1959¹⁶.
'Der religionsgeschichtliche Hintergrund des Prologs zum Johannes-Evangelium.' *Eucharisterion, Festschrift für Hermann Gunkel*, vol. II. Göttingen, 1923.
Burney, C. F. *The Aramaic Origin of the Fourth Gospel*. Oxford, 1922.
Cerfaux, Lucien. 'L'hymne au Christ-Serviteur de Dieu (*Phil.*, II, 6–11 = *Is.*, LII, 13–LIII, 12).' *Miscellanea historica in honorem Alberti de Meyer*, vol. I. Louvain, 1946.
Colpe, Carsten. *Die religionsgeschichtliche Schule. Darstellung und Kritik ihres Bildes vom gnostischen Erlösermythus*. FRLANT, N.F. 60. Göttingen, 1961.
Colwell, Ernest Cadman. *The Greek of the Fourth Gospel*. Chicago, 1931.
Coptic Gnostic Papyri in the Coptic Museum at Old Cairo, vol. I. Ed. Pahor Labib. Cairo, 1956–.
Davies, W. D. *Paul and Rabbinic Judaism. Some Rabbinic Elements in Pauline Theology*. New York and Evanston, 1967².
Deichgräber, Reinhard. *Gotteshymnus und Christushymnus in der frühen Christenheit. Untersuchungen zu Form, Sprache und Stil der frühchrist-*

lichen Hymnen. Studien zur Umwelt des Neuen Testaments, 5. Göttingen, 1967.

De resurrectione (Epistula ad Rheginum). Edd. Michel Malinine *et al.* Zurich, 1963.

Dibelius, Martin. *An die Kolosser, Epheser, an Philemon.* HNT, 12. Tübingen, 1953³, rev. by Heinrich Greeven.

Die Pastoralbriefe. HNT, 13. Tübingen, 1955³, rev. by Hans Conzelmann.

Dodd, C. H. *The Interpretation of the Fourth Gospel.* Cambridge, 1953.

Dürr, Lorenz. *Die Wertung des göttlichen Wortes im Alten Testament und im Antiken Orient.* Mitteilungen der vorderasiatisch-aegyptischen Gesellschaft, XLII, 1. Heft. Leipzig, 1938.

Eltester, Friedrich-Wilhelm. *Eikon im Neuen Testament.* BZNW, 23. Berlin, 1958.

Evangelium Veritatis. Edd. Michel Malinine, Henri-Charles Puech, and Gilles Quispel. Zurich, 1956. Supplement, 1961.

Feuillet, A. 'L'hymne christologique de l'épître aux Philippiens (II, 6–11).' *RB,* vol. LXXII. 1965.

Funk, Robert W. *Language, Hermeneutic, and Word of God. The Problem of Language in the New Testament and Contemporary Theology.* New York and Evanston, 1966.

Georgi, Dieter. 'Der vorpaulinische Hymnus Phil 2, 6–11.' *Zeit und Geschichte, Dankesgabe an Rudolf Bultmann zum 80. Geburtstag.* Tübingen, 1964.

Die gnostischen Schriften des koptischen Papyrus Berolinensis 8502. Ed. Walter Till. Texte und Untersuchungen zur Geschichte der altchristlichen Literatur, 60. Berlin, 1955.

The Gospel According to Thomas. Edd. A. Guillaumont *et al.* New York, 1959.

Grant, Robert M. *Gnosticism and Early Christianity.* New York, 1959.

'Notes on Gnosis.' *VChr,* vol. XI. 1957.

'The Odes of Solomon and The Church of Antioch.' *JBL,* vol. LXIII. 1944.

Gressmann, Hugo. *Altorientalische Texte und Bilder zum Alten Testament,* vol. I: *Texte.* Berlin, 1926.

Gunkel, Hermann. 'Die Oden Salomos.' *ZNW,* vol. XI. 1910.

'Psalmen.' *RGG²,* vol. IV. Edd. Hermann Gunkel and Leopold Tzscharnack. Tübingen, 1930.

'Salomo-Oden.' *RGG²,* vol. V. Edd. Hermann Gunkel and Leopold Tzscharnack. Tübingen, 1931.

Haenchen, Ernst. 'Probleme des johanneischen "Prologs".' *ZThK,* vol. LX, 1963.

Harnack, Adolf. *Ein jüdisch-christliches Psalmbuch aus dem ersten Jahrhundert.* Texte und Untersuchungen, 35, 4. Leipzig, 1910.

Harris, Rendel, and Mingana, Alphonse. *The Odes and Psalms of Solomon*, vol. II. Manchester, 1920.

Héring, Jean. 'Kyrios Anthropos.' *RHPR*, vol. VI. 1936.

Jeremias, Joachim. *Die Briefe an Timotheus und Titus*. NTD, 9. Göttingen, 1947.

'Zur Gedankenführung in den Paulinischen Briefen.' *Studia Paulina in honorem Johannis de Zwaan*, edd. J. N. Sevenster and W. C. van Unnik. Haarlem, 1953.

Jervell, Jacob. *Imago Dei*. Göttingen, 1960.

Jonas, Hans. *The Gnostic Religion*. Boston, 1958.

Käsemann, Ernst, 'Aufbau und Anliegen des johanneischen Prologs.' *Libertas Christiana, Festschrift für Friedrich Delekat*. Beiträge zur Evangelischen Theologie, 26. Munich, 1957.

'Eine urchristliche Taufliturgie.' *Exegetische Versuche und Besinnungen, Gesammelte Aufsätze*, vol. I. Göttingen, 1960.

'Kritische Analyse von Phil. 2, 5–11.' *Exegetische Versuche und Besinnungen, Gesammelte Aufsätze*, vol. I. Göttingen, 1960.

Das wandernde Gottesvolk. Eine Untersuchung zum Hebräerbrief. FRLANT, N.F. 37. Göttingen, 1961[4].

Koptisch-gnostische Apokalypsen aus Codex V von Nag Hammadi im Koptischen Museum zu Alt-Kairo. Edd. Alexander Böhlig and Pahor Labib. *Wissenschaftliche Zeitschrift der Martin-Luther-Universität*. Halle-Wittenberg, Sonderband, 1963.

Die koptisch-gnostische Schrift ohne Titel aus Codex II von Nag Hammadi im Koptischen Museum zu Alt-Kairo. Edd. Alexander Böhlig and Pahor Labib. Deutsche Akademie der Wissenschaften zu Berlin, Institut für Orientforschung, 58. Berlin, 1962.

Kroll, Joseph. *Die christliche Hymnodik bis zu Klemens von Alexandreia. Verzeichnis der Vorlesungen an der Akademie zu Braunsberg im Sommer 1921*. Königsberg, 1921; reprinted Darmstadt, 1968.

Langdon, Stephen (ed.). *Sumerian and Babylonian Psalms*. Paris, 1909.

Lohmeyer, Ernst. *Die Briefe an die Philipper, an die Kolosser, und an Philemon*. Kritisch-exegetischer Kommentar über das Neue Testament. Göttingen, 1964[13].

Kyrios Jesus. Eine Untersuchung zu Phil. 2, 5–11. Sitzungsberichte der Heidelberger Akademie der Wissenschaften, Phil.-hist. Kl. Jahrgang 1927/8, 4. Abhandlung; reprinted Darmstadt, 1961.

MacRae, George W. 'The Coptic Gnostic Apocalypse of Adam.' *Heythrop Journal*, vol. VI. 1965.

Manson, William. *Jesus the Messiah. The Synoptic Tradition of the Revelation of God in Christ: With Special Reference to Form-Criticism*. London, 1943.

Martin, R. P. *Carmen Christi. Philippians ii. 5–11 in Recent Interpretation and in the Setting of Early Christian Worship.* SNTS Monograph Series, 4. Cambridge, 1967.

Moffatt, James. *A Critical and Exegetical Commentary on the Epistle to the Hebrews.* ICC. Edinburgh, 1924.

Moore, George Foot. *Judaism in the First Centuries of the Christian Era. The Age of the Tannaim,* vol. I. Cambridge, 1944.

Mowinckel, Sigmund. 'Psalms and Wisdom.' *Wisdom in Israel and in the Ancient Near East.* Supplements to *Vetus Testamentum,* 3. Leiden, 1955.

Nock, Arthur Darby. Review of *Gnosis und spätantiker Geist, Teil I* (1934), by Hans Jonas. *Gnomon,* vol. XII. 1936.

Norden, Eduard. *Agnostos Theos.* Stuttgart, 1956⁴.

Die Oden Salomos. Ed. Walter Bauer. Kleine Texte für Vorlesungen und Übungen, 64. Berlin, 1933.

Pokorný, Petr. 'Epheserbrief und gnostische Mysterien.' *ZNW,* vol. LIII. 1962.

Preisendanz, Karl. 'Tammuz.' *Paulys Real-Encyclopädie der classischen Altertumswissenschaft,* 2. Reihe, vol. IV, 2. Edd. Wilhelm Kroll and Karl Mittelhaus. Stuttgart, 1932.

Reicke, Bo. *The Disobedient Spirits and Christian Baptism. A Study of I Peter 3:19 and its Context.* Acta seminarii neotestamentici upsaliensis, 13. Copenhagen, 1946.

Reitzenstein, Richard. *Das iranische Erlösungsmysterium.* Bonn am Rhein, 1921.

'Das mandäische Buch des Herrn der Grösse und die Evangelienüberlieferung.' *Sitzungsberichte der Heidelberger Akademie der Wissenschaften,* Phil.-hist. Kl. Jahrgang 1919, 12. Abhandlung.

Zwei religionsgeschichtliche Fragen nach ungedruckten griechischen Texten der Strassburger Bibliothek. Strassburg, 1901.

Ringgren, Helmer. *Word and Wisdom. Studies in the Hypostatization of Divine Qualities and Functions in the Ancient Near East.* Lund, 1947.

Robinson, James M. 'A Formal Analysis of Colossians 1:15–20.' *JBL,* vol. LXXVI. 1957.

'Die Hodajot-Formel in Gebet und Hymnus des Frühchristentums.' *Apophoreta, Festschrift für Ernst Haenchen.* BZNW, 30. Berlin, 1964.

Ruckstuhl, E. *Die literarische Einheit des Joh-Ev.* Studia Friburgensia, N.F. 3. Freiburg in der Schweiz, 1951.

Rudolph, Kurt. Review of *Koptisch-gnostische Apokalypsen aus Codex V von Nag Hammadi. ThLZ,* vol. XC. 1965.

'War der Verfasser der Oden Salomos ein "Qumran-Christ"? Ein Beitrag zur Diskussion um die Anfänge der Gnosis.' *Revue de Qumran,* vol. IV. 1963–4.

Sanders, Jack T. 'Hymnic Elements in Ephesians 1–3.' *ZNW*, vol. LVI. 1965.

Schenke, Hans-Martin (ed.). 'Das Evangelium nach Philippus.' *ThLZ*, vol. LXXXIV. 1959.

Der Gott 'Mensch' in der Gnosis. Göttingen, 1962.

Die Herkunft des sogenannten Evangelium Veritatis. Göttingen, 1959.

(ed.). 'Vom Ursprung der Welt. Eine titellose Abhandlung aus dem Funde von Nag Hamadi.' *ThLZ*, vol. LXXXIV. 1959.

(ed.). 'Das Wesen der Archonten.' *ThLZ*, vol. LXXXIII. 1958.

Schille, Gottfried. *Frühchristliche Hymnen.* Berlin, 1962.

Schlier, Heinrich. *Der Brief an die Epheser.* Düsseldorf, 1962³.

Christus und die Kirche im Epheserbrief. Beiträge zur historischen Theologie, 6. Tübingen, 1930.

'Die Kirche nach dem Brief an die Epheser.' *Die Kirche im Epheserbrief.* Beiträge zur Kontroverstheologie, 1. Münster-Westfalen, 1949.

'κεφαλή, ἀνακεφαλαιόομαι', *TDNT*, vol. III, ed Gerhard Kittel, trans. and ed. Geoffrey W. Bromiley. Grand Rapids, Michigan, 1965.

Schnackenburg, Rudolf. 'Logos-Hymnus und johanneischer Prolog.' *Biblische Zeitschrift*, vol. I. 1957.

Schulz, Siegfried. 'Salomo-Oden.' *RGG*³, vol. V. Ed. Kurt Galling. Tübingen, 1961.

Schweizer, Eduard. 'Aufnahme und Korrektur jüdischer Sophia-theologie im Neuen Testament.' *Hören und Handeln, Festschrift für Ernst Wolf.* Munich, 1962.

Erniedrigung und Erhöhung bei Jesus und seinen Nachfolgern. Abhandlungen zur Theologie des Alten und Neuen Testaments, 28. Zurich, 1962².

'Die Kirche als Leib Christi in den paulinischen Antilegomena.' *ThLZ*, vol. LXXXVI. 1961.

Scroggs, Robin. *The Last Adam. A Study in Pauline Anthropology.* Philadelphia, 1966.

Sellin, Ernst and Fohrer, Georg. *Einleitung in das Alte Testament.* Heidelberg, 1965¹⁰.

Selwyn, Edward Gordon. *The First Epistle of St Peter.* London, 1946.

Spicq, C. *L'Épître aux Hébreux.* 2 vols. Études Bibliques. Paris, 1952, 1953.

Spitta, Friedrich. 'Zum Verständnis der Oden Salomos.' *ZNW*, vol. XI. 1910.

Stanley, David M. 'The Theme of the Servant of Yahweh in Primitive Christian Soteriology and its Transposition by St Paul.' *CBQ*, vol. XVI. 1954.

Strecker, Georg. 'Redaktion und Tradition im Christushymnus Phil 2, 6–11.' *ZNW*, vol. LV. 1964.

van Unnik, W. C. *Evangelien aus dem Nilsand*. Trans. by Jean Landré. Frankfurt am Main, 1960.

'The "Gospel of Truth" and the New Testament.' *The Jung Codex*. Ed. F. L. Cross. London, 1955.

Westermann, Claus. *Das Loben Gottes in den Psalmen*. Göttingen, 1961².

Wilckens, Ulrich. *Weisheit und Torheit*. Beiträge zur historischen Theologie, 26. Tübingen, 1959.

Wilson, R. McL. 'Gnosis, Gnosticism and the New Testament.' *Le origini dello Gnosticismo. Colloquio di Messina*. Studies in the History of Religions (Supplements to *Numen*), 12. Leiden, 1967.

Windisch, Hans. 'Die göttliche Weisheit der Juden und die paulinische Theologie.' *Neutestamentliche Studien Georg Heinrici*. Untersuchungen zum Neuen Testament, 6. Leipzig, 1914.

Witzel, P. Maurus. *Tammuz-Liturgien und Verwandtes*. Analecta Orientalia, 10. Rome, 1935.

Ziener, P. Georg. *Die theologische Begriffssprache im Buche der Weisheit*. Bonner biblische Beiträge, 11. Bonn, 1956.

Zimmerli, W. and Jeremias, J. *The Servant of God*. Trans. by Harold Knight *et al*. Studies in Biblical Theology, 20. Naperville, Illinois, 1957.

Zimmern, Heinrich. 'Der babylonische Gott Tamūz'. *Abhandlungen der königlich-sächsischen Gesellschaft der Wissenschaften*. Philolog.-hist. Kl. Jahrgang 1909, no. 27.

'Babylonische Hymnen und Gebete in Auswahl.' *Der Alte Orient*, vol. VII, no. 3. 1905.

I. INDEX OF PASSAGES CITED

A. OLD TESTAMENT

C. OTHER LITERATURE FROM ANTIQUITY

(Including Apocrypha and Pseudepigrapha)

II. INDEX OF MODERN AUTHORS